BIBLICAL HOMILIES

KARL RAHNER

BIBLICAL HOMILIES

HERDER AND HERDER

1966
HERDER AND HERDER NEW YORK
232 Madison Avenue, New York, N. Y. 10016

Original edition:
"Biblische Predigten", Herder, Freiburg, 1965
Translated by:
Desmond Forristal and Richard Strachan

Nihil obstat: Joannes M. T. Barton, S.T.D., L.S.S.
                Censor deputatus

Imprimatur: † Patritius Casey,
               Vic. Gen.
               Westmonasterii, die 24a Maii 1966.

The *Nihil obstat* and *Imprimatur* are a declaration that a book or pamphlet is considered to be free from doctrinal or moral error. It is not implied that those who have granted the *Nihil obstat* and *Imprimatur* agree with the contents, opinions or statements expressed.

Library of Congress Catalog Card No. 66-2486.
First published in West Germany © 1966, Herder KG
Printed in West Germany by Herder

FOREWORD

Karl Rahner has asked me to say a few words by way of introduction to this book. For nearly ten years he preached Sunday after Sunday in the university church at Innsbruck, mostly on biblical texts. From time to time somebody would take down these sermons in shorthand, but they were not designed to be taken down or subsequently published. Since we do have a certain number of them in writing, however, they may provide useful reading and meditation for many people. Despite all the changes that have taken place in the Church and the world, these sermons still speak as forcefully as ever to the individual. There is no artificiality about them. Without any show of knowledge, they attempt to bring the age-old, familiar texts home to men here and now; to those who are prepared to listen and to admit their shortcomings; to those who will not take fright at simple, concrete demands—for these sermons do not speak the language of easy optimism—, to those who will let mystery show them their true selves, who are prepared to understand that to be Catholic is to be brotherly. All of which means that these words are worth preserving in print. The forty-five sermons selected by agreement with Karl Rahner from the years

1953 to 1958 do not make up a complete "liturgical year" or cover a cycle of subjects. So it seemed appropriate to arrange them according to the sequence of biblical books, while indicating in each case the relevant day of the ecclesiastical year.

Herbert Vorgrimler

CONTENTS

FOR US NO ANGEL FROM HEAVEN

Mt 1:18–21

(Feast of St Joseph, 19 March)

We are going to consider the text of scripture which the Church sets before us on this feast-day. It consists of four verses from the first chapter of St Matthew. We know it well, we have often read it and heard it read. The story is one which we remember from our Bible history class in school. And yet, though it is so familiar to us all, it poses us quite a problem, not in its deeper theological meaning but simply in what it tells about the outward events in the lives of St Joseph and the Blessed Virgin. We shall not be able to solve the problem fully. The text will remain obscure. Yet it may be that this very obscurity, when we study it more closely, may suggest thoughts that will deepen the text for us and be of significance for our own lives.

Usually we take this story to mean that Joseph had some inkling of the fact that Mary was with child but was quite at a loss for an explanation, that Mary remained silent about what the angel had told her and about what had happened to her through the power of the Most High, and that Joseph in his perplexity could think of no other course than to send her away, though she was betrothed to him. All this may well be correct, but we cannot say that it is the only possible interpretation of the text. For it begins by saying that Mary "was found to be with child of the Holy Spirit". This implies that Joseph knew that she had conceived by the Holy Spirit. How could he have come to know this? We must conclude that he can only have learned it from Mary and we ask why in that case she did not tell him also about the heavenly apparition and about God's gracious action in her regard. Why should she, the calm and devout servant of God, fail to tell him, her betrothed, about these things? Did she think, could she have thought, that Joseph could have learned them from some other source? Why should she assume without any evidence that Joseph too had received a message from heaven, when it would be so much simpler for her to tell him? And if Joseph knew of the miraculous favour bestowed on his bride, how could he ever have thought of putting her away privately? Conversely we can ask: if Joseph did not know that her child had been conceived miraculously, how could he, described here as a "just man", that is to say, a law-abiding man, have contemplated putting her away privately? He was bound in accordance with the law as set down in the 22nd chapter of the Fifth Book of Moses to proceed against her as against an adulteress. And if we answer: No, he must have known, it says here in the text too that he knew, why then should he have wanted to put her away at all?

Could it have been perhaps for this reason that he felt himself, was bound to feel himself, somehow shut out from this mystery which had come to pass between Mary and heaven? Since she had now been claimed by someone higher, indeed by God himself, we may well suppose that Joseph felt he could have no further claim of any kind upon her and resolved, therefore, to put her away privately.

If we interpret the text in this way—and it is at least a

possible interpretation of an obscure and difficult text—then the message that Joseph received from heaven, the angel that appeared to him in a dream, takes on a new and different light. The angel does not merely tell Joseph that Mary has conceived her child through the power of God—though this fact, which Joseph already knew from Mary, is confirmed by the apparition—but has as his principal message: "Take Mary your wife". Be a father to this child, heaven is saying, fulfil the duties of a father towards this child which heaven has sent to your bride. Protect, watch over, love, shield, take care of this child. This duty is laid on Joseph by God himself. We can say, therefore, that he is the foster-father and guardian of the child, not just because his wedded bride has conceived a child from heaven, but because God himself wished him to take the place of a father to the Son of God who has come to save the world. This is why Joseph is told to give a name to the child, this is why Joseph is addressed as "Son of David" since Jesus himself will be known and acknowledged as the son of David precisely because his earthly father is a son of David stemming from that royal lineage. Thus from our reading of this text we can see heaven entrusting to the care of Joseph the saviour of the world. Through this message from above Joseph is drawn into the great, public, official story of salvation. He acts no longer in the purely private capacity of bridegroom and later husband of Mary, but plays an official role in the salvation story. He is the guardian and protector of the Son of God, directly appointed to that office, and not just drifting into this relationship with the divine child through the accident of his betrothal to Mary.

We too are often called to be guardians of the Holy One in ourselves, in our lives, in our work. At first sight, our every-day affairs may seem to have nothing to do with the history of the kingdom of God and the salvation of the world. We may seem to be concerned with nothing more than the tissue of relationships that makes up our lives, our friendships, our work. But even here we are being called upon to be the guardians of something holy, something great, God's grace in us and about us. Is there anyone who has not some of God's children entrusted to his care: in the home, in the school, in the neighbourhood? For us no angel from heaven appears, no dream apparition bids us: Take the child to yourself. And yet it seems as though through purely earthly incidents we are made responsible for what is heavenly and divine, for God's grace in our own hearts and in our earthly surroundings. In all these the Son of God who became man continues his life, and we are all asked whether the task of guarding this Son of God whom we meet in others will find us as true as Joseph, of whom it is said: he was faithful, he took the child and his mother to himself, he spent his whole life guarding the child so that it might become in truth the saviour and the life of the world.

HE CAME ON THE SIDE OF THE WEAK

Mt 4:1–11

(First Sunday in Lent)

The Gospel tells us what came as the result of Jesus's fast in the desert—his temptation by the devil. Its place in our Lord's life is at the beginning of his messianic activity. Before he begins to announce the kingdom of God that has come in his person, before he begins to preach, he prays. Before he appears in public, he goes into the wilderness. Before he mingles with the multitude, he enters the solitude. Before he seeks out men, he first seeks the face of his Father in heaven. And he fasts.

Jesus is truly a man and, because he is truly an historical man, everything he does or suffers must reveal and make concrete all that flows from his union with the eternal Word of God in his human nature. Although he is always in that which is his Father's, although his soul in its depths is always united in prayer with the eternal God, there are times in the life of Jesus when this hidden union with God is realized in what might be called an express and deliberately willed prayer. Therefore Jesus goes into the desert, therefore he fasts, therefore he leaves behind everything else that a man needs even for bare existence, so that for this once not just in the depths of his heart but in the whole range of his being he can do and say what is the first and last duty of mankind—to find God, to seek God, to belong to God to the exclusion of everything else that makes up the life of man. And therefore he fasts. Therefore through this cruelly hard act, this denial of all comfort, this refusal of food and drink, through the solitude and abandonment of the desert, through everything else that involves a rejection, a self-denial of the world and all earthly company, through all these he proclaims this fact: one thing only is necessary, that I be with God, that I find God, and everything else, no matter how great or beautiful, is secondary and subordinate and must be sacrificed, if needs be, to this ultimate movement of heart and spirit.

In this desert of solitary prayer, Jesus is tempted. If we look more closely at these three temptations of our Lord, we see that in all three the devil seized on the apparent discrepancy between what Jesus knew about himself and what he was so immediately experiencing. Jesus knew that he was the Son of God. On this the devil—however we are to conceive him—fastened. If you are the Son of God, he says, then you should not be hungry, you should not be unheeded, you should not be powerless. And in truth, if a man knows that he is the blessed Son of God, if he knows that he is not merely surrounded by God's loving grace but is so caught up in the whole of his human reality, so gripped in the depths of his being, that everything felt or known or experienced there is truly the reality of the eternal Word of God—is it possible that he should suffer hunger or thirst, that he should find himself in misery in the midst of a terrifying solitude and abandonment, where there is no one to care about him, where he is so pitifully poor and lonely and abandoned, where no one notices him, while elsewhere the world makes its din and convinces itself of its own importance and goes about its business without any reference to him? Can he be reduced to such poverty and powerlessness that he has not even a piece of bread, that he can command nothing, that he has no one to minister to him? Is it possible that the kingdoms of the world with all their power and splendour should recede so far into the distance as to leave him all alone, insignificant, poor, hungry, and weak? So the devil plays on this discrepancy between what Jesus knows himself to be in his true inmost reality and what he is experiencing in his hunger, in his neglect, in his weakness, and says to him: Take firm hold of your inmost reality and make your protest from there; say that there must be bread, that attention must be paid to you, that the kingdoms and the power of the world must belong to you.

And what does Jesus do? He once again abandons, so to speak, his awareness of his divinity and takes his place on the side of the poor, the abandoned, and the weak. He does not answer the temptation by saying: I am the Son of God indeed, but it is fitting that he should be alone and hungry and weak. He says only what any man could say: that, though he is hungry, he wishes to live on the bread of God, that one must not tempt God, that one must serve God. That one must do what all of us men must do: resign ourselves to the reality that falls to our lot, even to poverty, even to loneliness, even to weakness. In this way the Son, reminded of his divine soneship by the powers of hell, embraces the common lot of us all, poverty, loneliness, the demands of God's service. He begins his messianic mission, in which not just in the depths of his being but in the action of his heart he strides across the infinite gulf that separates God from the creature, and finds himself where we are, the poor and weak, and lonely and abandoned, he to whom the devil had said: If you are the Son of God.

Since we are men and not the devil, we must say: If you are the Son of God, then you must be a son of man like ourselves, for our burden of toil and suffering can only be lifted if you act with us and desire nothing other than to share in our lot.

If we learn from this believing, hoping, loving stride across everything merely of this world that we are children of God, if we accept all the more willingly what falls to our lot, whether it be poverty or loneliness or the inability to change the world around us, then we are truly following Christ, then we are surrounded by God's grace and love, then God speaks to us with that power which can never leave us lonely and abandoned, and says: You are my son, I have loved you with an everlasting love.

IN TWO WAYS HUMBLED

Mt 8: 1–13

(Third Sunday after Epiphany)

The eighth chapter follows immediately after the Sermon on the Mount and, together with the ninth chapter, forms a section in which St Matthew sets a seal on the Sermon by relating some of the Lord's miracles, the cure of the leper and the healing of the centurion's servant at Capharnaum. We shall consider the second of these two miracles and in order to deepen our understanding of the story of the centurion of Capharnaum beyond the merely miraculous aspect, we shall have to look a little more deeply into the background.

Capharnaum was a border town between the territories of Philip and Herod Antipas, who had divided between them the kingdom of their father Herod. As a border town it had a customs post, where we meet Matthew, and a garrison. We know from the Gospels and also from the literature of the time that the troops of Herod Antipas consisted for the most part of pagans. Thus it happened, as we see more clearly from the seventh chapter of St Luke, where the first ten verses recount the same incident, that this centurion was a pagan and a foreigner, a man who was a member of the occupying forces, a man who was cut off by his culture, his politics, and his religion from the people of the place. We might describe him in the language of the Gospels as a man who did not belong to the children of the kingdom, who was not one of those to whom the Judaism of that time would allow any right to the promises of God or who was subject to the law of the living God. He was one of those who stood outside. That is how the Jews of the time must have looked on the centurion and they must have disapproved of him all the more since he was not only a heathen but, as we have said before, a representative of the forces of oppression. That is one side of the picture.

On the other side, we learn in the seventh chapter of St Luke that this centurion had showed himself very friendly towards the Jewish people. There the Jews themselves say about him: He loves our nation. And there is something more they can tell the Lord in his favour, something which hardly seems to match with the status of a junior officer, one who commanded a century, the smallest military unit of the time. He built our synagogue, they say, the synagogue of Capharnaum, the synagogue where Jesus preaches his wonderful promise of the bread of life in the sixth chapter of St John. This centurion had also undoubtedly a sympathetic under-standing of the Jews, of their religion, their promises, their expectation of a coming kingdom of God to be ushered in by the Messiah. But while he sympathized, he knew he did not belong to their nation. He shows his respect for this dividing line by a simple but significant gesture. A Jew never entered the house of a pagan unless he had to. The centurion knew this. He did not resent it. And therefore he said to the Lord: I am not worthy to have you come under my roof. This is not so much the expression of a personal humility in face of the contrast between his private person and the Lord, the wonder-worker, radiant with holiness and greatness. It is rather the gesture of humility of a man who carefully regards the religious views of another, who as a matter of course and with what one might call the tolerance of humility takes into account the mentality of another, respects it, refrains from wounding it—even, it may be, at the expense of his own feelings. So with reverence and respect for the Jewish people, but with respect also for the distance that separated him from them, the centurion looked on Jesus and believed in him, believed in the dignity of his person, believed in his claim, believed in his power to work miracles in proof of his mission. He is also a man who stands faithfully by his servants. So he sends the leaders of the synagogue—this we learn from St Luke's account, fuller and more accurate than St Matthew's—to ask the Lord for a miracle, the curing of his servant.

The Gospel story emphasizes the wonder and astonishment of Jesus at this faith. One might almost say that the centurion's attitude is matched by a similar attitude on the part of Jesus, but on a divine scale. He also is the child of his people. He also respects the limitations imposed on his earthly life, for he knows that he is sent primarily only to his people, to the lost sheep of the house of Israel. And in St John's Gospel he says that salvation comes from the Jews. Hence: "Truly, I say to you, not even in Israel have I found such faith." This practical demonstration, evidently genuine and spontaneous, that outside the people of God, outside the covenant, outside what was for hundreds and thousands of years the special field of God's activity, there existed more faith, more loyalty, more respect for what was good and valuable, this single demonstration is broadened by Jesus to the extent of saying that many will come from east and west and from north and south—as St Luke adds—and sit down with Abraham and Isaac and Jacob in the kingdom of God at that everlasting divine banquet, while the sons of the kingdom, those who thought that their descent from Father Abraham would give them a right to this eternal kingdom of God, are thrown into the outer darkness, where there will be weeping and gnashing of teeth. It is clear that for St Matthew the whole point of the miracle is that it was worked on behalf of someone who did not belong to the chosen people, since he includes in his narrative this saying of the Lord which Luke in his thirteenth chapter assigns to an entirely different and more likely occasion.

Does all this not have some meaning for us? It is certainly possible that we could fail to put a high enough value on the grace of Christ found in the Church, but it is also possible that we could fall into the opposite error of thinking that we alone are the chosen ones, we who are inside, the sons of the kingdom. Jesus by his example is saying this to us: You must be the kind of men who will not hesitate to recognize the truth, to recognize goodness, honesty, virtue, loyalty, courage, wherever they appear. You must not be party men. You must see the light wherever it shines. It may be anywhere, without prejudice to the truth of the Church. We know from our faith that God's grace is not confined to the visible Church of Christ, that God's grace comes and goes through all the alleyways of the world and finds everywhere hearts in which supernatural salvation is wrought through this faith and this grace. So we Catholics should not fall into the mistake of thinking that, because we are the children of the true Church, there can be no divine grace or love except in our hearts. We must be told again and again what this Gospel tells us, that the children of the kingdom can be among those cast out, while others who did not seem to be chosen will come from the four corners of the earth and be numbered among the elect. The grace of the true Church should make us feel humbled in two ways. First because we must admit to ourselves that we are perhaps not all that we could be if this grace were fully alive and true in us. Secondly, because it brings us no certain guarantee of election. So let us follow the example of the Lord and be open and generous in recognizing whatever is good, whatever is noble and active and admirable and alive, wherever it may be, in recognizing that grace can work also outside the visible Church. Let the grace we have received make us all the more humble and so prepare us to enjoy its fruits in eternity.

THE DENARIUS STANDS FOR US
—AND FOR GOD

Mt 20:1–16

(Septuagesima)

It seems to me that this Gospel of the labourers in the vineyard, even though we know it so well, appears stranger and more incomprehensible each time it is read. That every man receives the same reward surely does not hold true of eternity. Nor can we conclude from this story that God does not render to every man according to his works, for it is written in scripture that he does. What then, we may well ask, is this story really telling us?

We have here a parable of the Lord that demonstrates what is true of all his parables, namely that one must concentrate on the message of the story as a whole and not try to find an application for every detail of the story in the religious and supernatural sphere, in the relationship of man to God. In this parable we should not ask who those are who were called at the first hour and those who were called at the third, sixth, ninth, and eleventh hours. We should not seek any special significance in the fact that the lastcomers were paid first or in other similar details. At God's eternal judgement there will be no grumblers. All these details in Jesus's story were put in only to throw into relief the central message, which is all that really matters. But what is this central message?

To understand the parable we must remember in the first place that at that time the usual wage of a hired labourer was one denarius for one day's work. So when the householder offered one denarius to those who were willing to work in his vineyard and who went and did the work, and when he had them paid a denarius at the end of the day, he was giving them the wage that was normal, accepted, fair, and—to use modern teminology—in accordance with social justice. They have no reason to be surprised at it. When they started the day they expected no more. Therefore it is clear that when the householder has a denarius paid out to each of the latecomers, there is no longer question of a wage which they have earned. He had not even promised them this denarius, for all he said was that he would give them what was right. And they certainly did not expect to be given so much. The householder expressly asks the grumblers whether he has not the right to be generous. What he gives to these latecomers, therefore, is not an expression of wages which they have earned or of the justice which applies to masters and servants; rather it is an expression of his own generosity, that free generosity—and here we are coming to the point of the whole story—that incalculable mercy, that grace which cannot be reckoned up in terms of wages and justice, that generosity and mercy which ultimately prevails between God and man. This story does not deal with the question whether any man is rewarded by God's judgement according to his works or not. In this parable Jesus is saying something else, something far wider, something especially significant in view of the way in which the Jews of that time were preoccupied with rewards; he is saying to us that between God and us there prevails something quite different, something that cannot be calculated, that cannot be expressed in terms of justice, something that is in fact the mercy and free disposition of the eternal God. This is a truth which at first humbles a man, for it tells him that he is not someone who can confront God with claims in justice which he has established through his own efforts. He is not someone who can calculate with God. But this truth, that everything depends on the free mercy of God, is also a truth which comforts us and raises us up and frees us from a burden. For if we were to calculate with God, then God would calculate with us and question our claim. In that case we would inevitably come off second-best. No, it is certainly better that everything should depend on God's free mercy. For it means that whether we begin to serve God early or late, we can always be of good heart, and no matter what demands are made upon us, we can say to God: You are the God of mercy and consolation, the God who bestows grace and who makes payment with the denarius that no one can earn by his own efforts, who makes payment to us who are such poor sinners and unprofitable servants.

Where it is that this mercy of God enters our life, where it is that he shows himself to us as one freely disposes of us and does not negotiate, is an entirely different question. We cannot find the answer to it in this parable. We cannot make an unjustified application of the details of this parable to the divine reality. We can only say that in the last analysis everything we can earn and must earn in the way of wages depends on the free disposition of God, who gives to us as he wills and ordains our beginning and our ending according to his pleasure. From this there follows something which can never, I think, lose its importance for us.

The thing which God freely disposes of, the thing we cannot negotiate or calculate about with him, is ultimately our own selves. Our own selves, just as we are: with our life, with our temperament, with our destiny, with our surroundings, with our time, with our heredity, with our family, with everything that we happen to be and cannot change. And whenever we grumble and complain about others with whom God has dealt differently, we are really refusing to accept our own selves from the hands of God. This parable teaches us to say: we are those who receive the denarius, we ourselves are the denarius. For we receive ourselves, with our destiny, with our freedom certainly and whatever we choose to do with that freedom, but ultimately what we receive is ourselves. This we must accept, not just without grumbling, without inward protest, but with a good will, because it is given to us by the God who asks: "Do you begrudge my generosity?" This, then, is our great life's work: to accept ourselves as the mysterious and gradually revealed gift of the eternal generosity of God. For everything that we are and have, even the painful and mysterious, is God's generous gift; we must not grumble at it but must accept it in the knowledge that when we do so God gives himself with his gift—here again the parable falls short of the reality—and so gives us everything that we could receive. To do this is the wisdom and the chief work of a Christian life. If we look into our own lives we will find that we have not always done it. All of us, young and old alike, are really latecomers. And yet God is willing to give us everything if we will only accept it—ourselves and himself and life without end.

THE CHRISTIAN AND THE INEVITABLE

Mt 24:15–35

(Last Sunday after Pentecost)

We are at the end of another year of the Church's time and another year of our own. Therefore at this time we should give thanks to God—and not just for this grace. For he has also kept us in the kingdom of his Son. He has preserved the light of faith for us and he has not taken his love from us and so this year has passed to the glory of God. What seems over and done with has been laid up in the future for us by God's mercy.

It is no accident that the Church reads in today's Gospel the passage that comes in the 24th chapter of St Matthew, verses 15 to 35. It is part of the Lord's discourse about the future and last things. In a mysterious way the discourse mingles the end of the world with the destruction of Jerusalem. Whether this is to be ascribed to the author of the Gospel or to the Lord himself is not of fundamental importance. For in spite of it we can see clearly the distinction between the two.

Verses 15 to 28 deal with the destruction of Jerusalem and the ending and abolition of the part played by the Old Covenant in the history of salvation.

Verses 29 to 31 deal with the Second Coming. Earlier the ending of the Old Testament salvation history was spoken of, now the ending of salvation history as a whole is described. It is not strange that the two are surveyed at the same time. Not that there is not an immeasurable length of time between the two, but still they belong together in their inner theological sense. In verses 32 to 35 questions about the timing of the first named events are dealt with. And about the end of Jerusalem we are told: "This generation will not pass away till all these things take place." And the question about the timing of the absolute ending of the history of salvation is answered when we are told that no one knows it except the Father himself. So already from these two answers we can see that the Lord draws a distinction in time between two events. Generally these sayings about the last things are regarded as though the Lord were here showing his powers of prophecy. But I think that these words (verses 15 to 28) can be looked at in another light. These words foretell times of historical catastrophe. But the prophecy is not made merely to show that the Lord knew all these things beforehand and that we too had some knowledge of them; rather he is giving rules by which a man is to conduct himself in such times of catastrophe. This too contains useful lessons for us. He is saying something obvious, which men nevertheless ignore. They should know the signs of the time, they should not turn their gaze from the historical situation, they should draw all the radical consequences; namely, that he who is in the field should not turn back, that he who is outside the house should not go for his mantle. Naturally not all of this applies to our case. But can we not also say that we should not deny the soundness of the earthly instinct? What then is our situation? Is it not true that everything is dark in our time, full of direst catastrophe, with all the talk about war and destruction? And yet we look away from it all and try to arrange our lives again in domestic comfort. We do not want to be men who have been told in what kind of times they live. We do not want to be men who draw the Christian consequences. Or are we men who remind ourselves that we must trust in God in this time of ours, that we must live from the deepest source of our being—in God and in our hope in him and in our love for him? If we saw our situation clearly, we would not fear catastrophe but we would be patient and resigned in doing and suffering whatever each day might bring us. We could do what has to be done in spite of the future: we could do our duty and whatever the present demands of us without heeding the threats of the future.

This question can be understood only by the man who believes and has confidence that God is the future and he alone.

The second thing of which Jesus reminds us in this text is prayer: pray, he says, that your flight may not be on a sabbath. Once again the command is not applicable in its context. But the Lord is foretelling a future which he says will be full of terror and in which part of the history of God's love is swallowed up in God's anger. He foresees inevitable catastrophes, he foresees them with resignation, and he tells us that prayer will still have its meaning there. How infinitely powerful he considers prayer to be, how realistically he appraises its effect! He says: These things will happen. He does not say: You can prevent them. But he does say: Pray, because that alone makes sense. We cannot estimate the possibilities of the future and we do not know what earthly results this prayer may achieve and what is denied to it by God's will. It is for us to trust in God and to pray also for an earthly future. If in an earthly situation a great deal is laid down as inevitable so that the Lord can say to us: This or that will happen and cannot be avoided—still we must listen to Christ's admonition in the Gospel, that prayer is still meaningful for history and even mandatory.

And the Lord says a third thing which follows from the others: For the sake of the elect those days will be shortened. For their sake: were it not for them, no one would be left alive in the whole area of this historical situation of which the Lord is speaking. He also tells us: There are elect. Here again he means: You cannot make a heaven on earth, you are not the representatives of a utopian dream future. But you are the blessing of God for this point of history and it will not be until the Last Judgement that we will be able to assess what the blessed of the Father in Heaven have meant for this point of history and for the ability to endure it. How often will we too say: For the sake of the elect these days have been shortened. So the Lord tells us with sober realism that, no matter what circumstances of catastrophe may exist, we can never have the right to believe only in the darkness of this earth. When they come, they must find us believing and loving, men who know that every trial is a pathway to God. God's word and God's power have laid on us the duty of becoming freely and willingly the elect for this our time. In the second century it was said: "For the sake of us Christians this era exists." The early Christians had this proud awareness of themselves. We have, must have, an equally strong belief in our own mission.

If we are persevering in faith, if we are the children of God and hence the children of his eternal election, then we should always pray with the hope that the days of darkness will be shortened. And always, whether we live or die, we must shine like stars in heaven. That is our duty, to act in the sight of God in heaven and of our historical age on earth in the way the Lord has told us to act: in sobriety and resolution, in prayer and in the awareness that we are the elect for whose sake the blessing and the promise have been given.

THE ETERNAL WORD OF GOD IS
OUR COMPANION AT TABLE

Mk 8:1–9

(Sixth Sunday after Pentecost)

When we listen to the Sunday Gospel we would do well to remember from time to time that it is being read during Holy Mass. The liturgy of the Word, including the proclaiming of the Gospel and its interpretation, is meant in the Holy Mass to form a part of this whole sacred event as well as being a preparation for the celebration of the Last Supper of Jesus, the holy sacrifice of the Church.

In the case of today's Gospel we must admit that many exegetes hold, seemingly with good reason, that this Gospel account of the multiplication of the loaves is not intended by the Evangelist to refer immediately to the eucharistic meal. But when we remember that at least St John explicitly regards the multiplication of the loaves as a holy and symbolic event pointing to the Last Supper, when we further observe that the writers of the synoptic Gospels depict Jesus in the same attitude as at the Last Supper, taking the bread, giving thanks, blessing it, breaking, and distributing it, then we should surely see in this account of the miracle of the loaves a foreshadowing of what we are to celebrate during this sacred time: the meal in which the Lord gives strength to his own in the desert of life through the hands of his apostles, so that they may not faint from weariness on their journey to eternity. Without drawing any far-fetched analogies or artificial allegories, we can still see that this Gospel is describing that relationship between Jesus and mankind that reaches its highest point and finds its deepest reality and truth in that bequest of the Lord, his Last Supper. Let us look a little closer at this Gospel. Jesus teaches in the desert but the word which he preaches and wishes to preach is really his revelation of himself as the kingdom of God's mercy come upon earth. Thus this word of Jesus tends directly to the end that what he reveals—namely, himself as the grace of God made flesh—enters really into the being of men, not just in thought but in all truth, in his spirit, in his grace, and in their historical manifestation, the sacraments and the Sacrament. And when these people are here in the desert, when they are in need, when Jesus himself says of them: "Some of them have come a long way", then all this is no more than one accidental manifestation and exemplification of the common condition of us all—that we are in need, that we cannot of ourselves provide the bread we need for our existence. We are those who are on a journey, we are those who have come a long way. We are those of whom Jesus has said: "I have compassion on the crowd." We are those who must endure long days with the Lord, and hunger also, until he takes pity on us and gives us strength. We must—like these people in the Gospel—listen to the word of God and listen again and again, until it really enters into us through the miracle of God's grace and becomes the strength of our lives and the light of our hearts. When Jesus gathers the apostles around him and makes them the instruments of his mercy to the people, he is calling them to be the foundations of his Church, the distributors of his grace, the preachers of his word. In this

Gospel he uses them as dispensers of the earthly bread and he will appoint them to dispense the heavenly bread to their brothers and sisters. Hence if we see in this activity of the apostles a foreshadowing of that future activity of theirs, which will be to join with the people of God in anticipating the feast of eternal life during this pilgrimage through time, we will not be straying too far from this Gospel and its primary meaning; for what happens in this Gospel is also intended by the Lord to happen today, at this particular hour, in this particular place.

The Lord is the centre of this event both here and in the Gospel: he takes the bread, he blesses it, he gives thanks to God for this gift of earth. He does it as the head of the household used to do it in the Old Testament, in the name of all those who were gathered around his table; but when the eternal Word of God prays to the Father in our flesh and as our companion at table, when he thanks him for the gifts of earth, blesses him and his name for all his mercy and love, then such an action performed by him who is Son of Man and Son of God has dimensions that are infinite: the eternal High Priest in the name of all his brothers and sisters offers the adoration of the world and of all history for ever and ever, while he offers himself through his death to the eternal Father. If the evangelists have stylized this Gospel scene in order to match the story of the Last Supper, then we in our turn can read into this Gospel what happens in our own lives: the Lord is in our midst as the great giver of thanks for us all, for our lives, for our destinies, and as the great offerer of sacrifice who includes us and our being in that great liturgy that embraces time and eternity and offers all things to God. If we go in faith to the table of the Lord, then we will be like the people of whom today's Gospel says: "They ate, and were satisfied." We will hunger all the more for the eternal banquet with God himself, we will be satisfied so that we will not faint on the way even though we have come from afar and the road to eternity is long. He gives himself to us, with his appointed death, with his cross; but also with the victory won by the cross which has saved us and our lives. This bread, which is he himself and which he offers to us, is the food of eternal life that gives strength for eternity. Through it there comes about what we see in the Gospel: a fellowship of pilgrims, a fellowship gathered around the apostles, a fellowship of a meal that includes everyone, a fellowship of one single pilgrim path to God. When we read this Gospel from the eighth chapter of St Mark, let us pray God to bring about in our midst and at this hour what is but faintly foretold and shadowed and promised by today's Gospel.

A MAN IS BORN

Lk 1:57–68

(Feast of the Nativity of St John the Baptist, 24 June)

What story is told in today's Gospel? A man is born. A mother rejoices. And the people around, parents, relations, friends, notice what happens in the case of every man and every birth because this birth is surrounded by strange circumstances which forces them to notice more clearly what takes place every time a man is born. In the first place we are told that these friends and relations rejoiced because God had shown his favour to this mother and hence also to this child. It is a favour when God calls a man into being, it is an act of grace, of love, of kindness, of unspeakable mercy. But is this all that obvious? Is our experience of ourselves, of our life, of our fortunes, of our reputation, so clearly such that we can praise and thank God for conferring a favour upon us? And yet it is so.

He has called us into existence, an existence that is ever-lasting. He has called us into his grace and this grace is he himself and his own eternal life. This existence, when we might never have existed, this eternity, behind which lies empty nothingness, this life with God and in his sight, which is given to the soul in grace and in glory, all this is a favour because it is the blessedness of God himself; and everything else in our lives, anything that may threaten this existence of ours, is transient and temporary, a test and a trial. What is given to us through human birth is a favour from God. Can we look on this life, with all its mystery, in this way and accept it day by day from the hands of God? Let us summon all the strength and all the courage at our command and say with joy: It is a favour!

The second thing which strikes us in this Gospel is the fact mentioned in the text that all around were seized with fear and anxiety on the occasion of this birth. But this fear is not a phobia, not a panicky and servile anxiety from which the Christian should be free since he is in the state of love and need not, as St John says, be afraid; the fear here spoken of is the fear of reverence in face of the fact of human existence. And all these people, who had witnessed the expectation of this child and had lived through the strange occurrences, thought: There is a mystery about this life. He who conferred this favour is the infinite God with all his unfathomable decrees and ordinances. He calls this man into being and no one can tell at the outset all that may be bound up with this call. Behind these lesser events they see the infinite mystery of God himself beginning to work through this incipient life, mysterious and inscrutable—and they are afraid. And still this fear is the fear of reverence, without which all human life and experience is a flat and empty commonplace. We are forever frantically trying to run away from this fear and find somewhere calmer, quieter and more comfortable, where this fear of God can no longer touch our lives. But whenever the course of our lives and divine decrees and ordinances teach us fear, then that fear is the fear of God and we are assured that it is blessed and that God loves and is faithful to those who fear him.

The third thing that strikes us in this Gospel comes at

the end. The father thanks God and praises him, saying: Blessed be the Lord God of Israel, for he has visited and redeemed his people. He utters a universal praise of all God's salvation history and includes the life of this child in his Benedictus canticle, this panoramic view of all that God has done for the salvation of mankind through his people and for all peoples. He gives thanks because this child, whom he has earlier addressed directly in the Benedictus, will be the precursor of the Lord who will prepare his way and make ready a perfect people for his God. This is something that can be said of everyone in his own way, of every one of us. A canticle could be sung for our lives, a hymn of thanksgiving, for we too belong to this chosen people whom God has called to follow his redeemer and to prepare a way before him into that future time which is always his. This is what the holy Eucharist, the holy prayer of thanksgiving of Christians, should say about our lives each Sunday.

There is a God, he has called us into existence without asking our leave, because he wished to confer this favour upon us. Ever since then the fearful and yet blessed mystery of God has ruled over the soul whom he has so called and thereby made himself to be the mystery of our lives. But over and over again and at all times we can say: Praised be God who has called us into fellowship with his Son, who has loved us and saved us and called us into his unspeakable light, who has made us to be among his followers, who himself as God has walked the pathways of our life, so that we could follow him and go before him to prepare his way, until the favour of God reveals itself as the ultimate meaning of the mystery of our life, until we can sing that eternal hymn of thanksgiving that shall not cease for ever.

LOVE SEES THE WORLD AS A PARABLE

Lk 5:1–11

(Fourth Sunday after Pentecost)

This story is found only in St Luke. Matthew and Mark merely state briefly that Jesus told Peter and his companions to follow him and become fishers of men, and that they followed. But Luke tells of an incident that preceded this call.

I think that in the case of this story we can do nothing better than read it in silence and recollection. It is a marvellous story. When we look at it, we are struck by how much is contained in these eleven verses. The sea is here and the land, the crowd and the individuals, the labour and the preaching of the word of God, the failure and the miraculous blessing on the renewed labour, the daily round of work and the call to a divine mission, the intimate familiarity of men with Jesus and the shiver of realization that he is the holy one and that we are sinners. We might say that this little incident contains everything, the whole of human life, all its reality, all its experience. Day and night are here, failure and success, bitterness and blessing. We are here and the Lord is here. And all these things are woven together in the quietest and most natural way. Each opens on to the other, one referring to another, none is as it were sealed off from the rest but every one relates to the whole and the whole is only the little things of everyday life preserved and confirmed and filled with blessing. This is not just an artificial impression. Something like this must have been in the mind of the Lord. He sees the boat and decides to teach from it. This certainly has a practical reason: it makes it easier for him to speak to the people who are pressing all around him. But it must also have occurred to him that it was Peter's ship he was going into. How else would he have come to see the calling of Peter under that figure of speech which here finds its reality: a fisherman on the sea?

Jesus himself sees all the incidents which are here joined to make a single whole. They are open to him and to his heart. This heart, which unites all things in its love, knows of no divisions. The fishing of these fishermen, who have caught nothing all night long, is so important to him that he crowns it with a miracle. If they here learned to labour the night long, catch nothing, and still obey the command of Jesus, they learned something for their new calling of fishers of men. Something like this will have to happen in us too and in our lives, which will have to find their unity in love. The unity of a love that despises nothing and shuts out nothing, the unity of a love that endures pettiness and remains open to greatness, a love that sees the world as a great parable, not a parable that is separate and apart, but a parable that is itself drawn into the great reality it represents. Our daily round of work is full of holy significance, a preparation for greatness. And it is in the midst of this daily round that what is holy happens. But in this relaxed, almost serene unity of the world, our lives, and our callings, only the man who is loving and patient can see and recognize the likeness of his own life. The man who hears the word of God from the midst of the crowd and feels that this word is addressed to him in the inmost solitude of his heart, the man who gratefully accepts the things of earth from the hand of God and knows himself to be loved by Christ in spite of everything, the man who says: "Depart from me for I am a sinful man", is the man who is called to the closest intimacy and the holiest imitation.

It seems to me that in this small incident in the life of Jesus, a few verses, we can read the secrets of our hearts and come to understand that all the love of the heart of Christ is found in one event: we are called, we follow, and in our failure we are blessed.

HOW POWERFUL IS THE SEED OF GOD?

Lk 8:4–15

(Sexagesima)

In the eighth chapter of St Luke we find the parable of the sower, as it is generally called. It could also be called the parable of the different fates of the word of God. This story must have been specially close to the heart of the primitive Church. It is found in all three synoptics: Mark has it in chapter 4 and Matthew in chapter 13. Scripture has also preserved for us the Lord's own explanation of the story. For that reason the preacher feels reluctant to add anything to these words of the Lord which are so clear. The parable is one that we understand at once.

If, however, we should desire to delve more deeply into this well-known parable, we might begin by asking ourselves why Jesus tells this parable and why he tells it to us. We could first ask ourselves why Jesus, seen in human terms, should have told this parable. We are entitled to think of the Lord in this truly human way because he is truly human. And therefore the things that he says come from his heart and reflect his inner feelings. If we ask why Jesus thus considered tells this parable we will have to answer: Because he cares so deeply about the fate of what he is speaking of. He comes, he speaks, he preaches, he distributes the words of God. They are strength, light,

grace, they come from his very heart. He is wholly involved
in what he says. He gives at the same time the full force of
his heart, his love, and his grace. He speaks from the source
of final and definitive words, because he comes from above
and does not speak human wisdom but proclaims that light
that comes down as God's grace and salvation on the
hearts of men to illumine them on their way to eternal light.
But when Jesus speaks and preaches in this way, what does
he see? His word is not accepted, he finds deaf ears and
cold hearts, he finds men who answer him with refusal,
with self-complacency, with contempt, with evasion. And
from the depths of his disappointment and the pain of this
experience, he asks: How is it that this word bears so little
fruit in this world? He tells himself the same parable that
he tells us: "A sower went out to sow his seed." He turns
his gaze to nature, to what his Father has made, to where
reality comes closest to what God had intended. He sees
that the seed that is sown there meets with different fates.
The end does not always correspond to the beginning.
Fashioned and given by the Father, it meets with different
fates, even though it was created by God—or perhaps
(who knows?) because it was created by God. This consoles him. This renews his courage to go on proclaiming
the message entrusted to him by his Father, to go on
working, to go on walking the fields of this world, sowing
the seed, tirelessly, patiently, persistently, to go on in all
weathers, no matter what fate the seed may meet, to leave
everything else to the decrees of the eternal Father, to the
mysterious providence of God.

We go on to ask our second question. Why does Jesus
tell this parable to us? Why does he tell us of what consoles
his heart? The answer must be that we are in danger of
taking scandal at what happens to God, to his grace, to

his Church, in ourselves, in history, in our surroundings, in everything we see. More, are we not tempted again and again to think that this cannot really be the seed of God, that it cannot be his word, his grace, his power, his design, his handwork, his Church, his sacrament, if the results it meets with are meagre, so wretched, so precarious, so continually rejected and destroyed by the world? Do we not keep asking ourselves—or are we afraid to ask ourselves—this question: Where is the finger of God to be found in our lives and in the history of our time? Do we not have the feeling that God's word should be more powerful, that God's power should be almighty in the history of our time, that God's light should shine more clearly in our hearts and in the world, that God's comfort and strength should more fully possess our poor, dry, cold, tired, dull hearts? Do we not, like Jesus, ask ourselves in our hearts: What are we to make of the fate of what claims to be the seed of God in this world, God's life and God's own fate?

Are we not then the kind of people to whom Jesus needs to tell this parable? But, we may ask, is this story then an answer to our question? Look: an answer to this question, if it is to be a true one, can only be given with diffidence, and silence would be a better answer still. Certainly Jesus tells us in the parable that it is not the seed of God that is at fault but the ground, the stony hearts, those who, in Jesus's words, spring up among thorns, among riches and pleasures—it is their fault that the life of God bears no fruit in dry and hardened hearts, in blind souls. But—one might be tempted to answer against this parable of the Lord—is all this not part of God's plan too? The stony hearts and the hard ground and the thorns and thistles of this world and the devil and the hard-trodden pathways of our time?

Is all this not foreseen and willed by God? Or if he merely permits it, is he not still responsible for it? We can easily be tempted to blame God for the different fates that the seed of God meets in the world.

If we are tempted in this way, then it is time to let this parable of Jesus speak to us, this parable told us by someone who knows God because he comes from him, for he himself has felt the pain of this question and the temptation of every human heart to cry out in protest. No, he tells us, each one of us, you must take the blame for the different fates of the word of God upon yourself, in your own heart, because you are a sinner, because you are hard of heart, because your soul does not seek after the light of God as it should be sought after. Only when you confess that you bear a responsibility for the fate of God and of his grace, a responsibility that cannot be removed or lessened or transferred or excused, only then will you be what you should be in the sight of God, only then will you find favour and justification with God. We must keep tilling the soil of our poor hearts, we must leave there no beaten track for the endless traffic of the world and its affairs to pass over, monotonous and incessant. We must prepare good soil in our hearts for the seed of God; and if we do this and ask for nothing more, then this seed of God will surely bring forth fruit in our hearts, thirtyfold and sixtyfold and a hundredfold. If we recognize our responsibility, we will see God in his mercy once more enabling us to be good soil for his seed. Then we will see that all is grace and the eternal mercy of God, who gives both the seed and the growth in his infinite generosity.

THE CHRISTIAN,
THE DEVIL AND CULTURE

Lk 11:14–18

(Third Sunday in Lent)

In today's Gospel, Jesus drives out a devil and heals a dumb man. Jesus regards this healing of a malady which had been caused by diabolical influence as a sign that the kingdom of God has come, a kingdom that cannot be divided, a kingdom that stands in diametrical opposition to everything that is of the devil, to everything diabolical and infernal. On the one hand, Jesus regards things which are of purely earthly significance, things like bodily health which concern purely earthly welfare, as subject to diabolical influence; and on the other hand, he regards what is right and good in this earthly dimension as a sign that the kingdom of God, the kingdom of eternity, has come. All this is clearly relevant to our theme.

We can state it quite simply. Even in this Gospel, which has no intention of expounding cultural-political principles, it clearly emerges that every man and every Christian has a cultural mission. Culture is taken here in the widest sense: everything in this earthly life that is worthy of human dignity, everything towards which man feels himself drawn or fitted in his history or in his concrete situation, through his spirit or through the forces of nature. Where-ever man makes something richer and more meaningful of his life, wherever he creates works of intellect, of science, of art, of literature, wherever he stamps the imprint of his spirit on the things of earth and expands his own being, there we find culture; and man is called to this by God not only for the reason, suggested in passing by today's Gospel, that he has powers given to him by God to be developed, but also quite clearly by virtue of the fact that he is a Christian. The Christian is the man of eternity, the man of God-given truth, the man who hears the word of the living God from beyond this world; the Christian is not just the man who prays: "Thy kingdom come" or "Let this world pass". The Christian is not just a man who is waiting for eternity and who looks on all earthly things as temporary; as a Christian he is a man sent into the world to carry out the earthly mission of his creator and Lord, the creator of heaven and earth. And why? So that everything that is good and wholesome, meaningful and upright, luminous and beautiful and complete and splendid on this earth is given to know, through this healing which routs the powers of darkness, that the kingdom of God is come.

This earthly culture is not of course itself the kingdom of God, but it is somehow a sign, a promise, a kind of sacramental sign that God loves this world, that he does not let it sink into the chaos of the diabolic, that he loves it, despite its sinfulness, in that same earthly structure which he gave it, that he guards it and cherishes it and enfolds it in the love of his creative will, and therefore that it is through his will that this particular world should exist, this culture, this spiritual universe of man. God himself with his eternal kingdom is coming into the darkness, so that it may become light, for faith tells us that there is something fundamentally sound, pure, true, and mature, some real culture, some genuine humanity that comes only from the grace of Christ, from the pierced heart of the Saviour, and, in consequence, that wherever this culture truly corresponds to the divine will and plan of creation, something more is present, and it shows forth God's grace in the sound humanity of this earth. That is why the Christian as such has always a cultural mission.

The second lesson which we can draw from this incidental meaning of today's Gospel is that this world is a divided world. It is not merely a creation of God that has perhaps failed to achieve its fully earthly perfection. This world in which culture, humanity, and the creative design of God are to be realized is also a world in which there is evil and darkness and hell. That is why man in all his creative activities, in all his earthly achievements and potentialities, in his literature and art and science and philosophy, is always liable to be seduced into falsity by the spirit of darkness, is always under the temptation to create a culture that is basically diabolical. That is why such a culture, such an earthly creation of man, must be exorcized and freed from all diabolical taint.

This is not entirely self-evident, as we know. We are in great danger of deceiving ourselves on this point. We tend to see the hand of the devil, the dark seductions of the abyss, only when we sin against the precepts of the book, against the express prohibitions of the ten commandments of God. And when we do not offend against these, then we think everything is in order, and we may easily find ourselves drifting with the tide, accepting as self-evident a "culture" that has been basically diabolized by the forces of debasement, by sheer luxury, by wild, senseless, form-less, and unhallowed sexuality, by the demons of covetous-ness and pride and self-imprisonment in things of earth—all this can easily happen. We can let ourselves think that because a thing is obvious, because it is widespread, because everybody does it, it must be right and proper. We can let ourselves think that because this debased culture is widespread it must be acceptable, because it is widespread it must be right and even becoming for us. And if we fight against it, we can let ourselves think that we are fighting in the name of what we call the old values, and thus be merely preserving what was evil yesterday against what is evil and earthly and thoroughly worldly today. It is not as easy as all that for us Christians, we cannot fulfil our cultural mission by just saying yes and amen to every current trend, neither can we content ourselves with an appeal to the past, for that too must be subject to a judgement, to a discernment of spirits. So it is not as easy as all that for the Christian in his task, in his mission to this world, and to present-day life. He must be a discerner of spirits. He must have the courage to say yes or no to both new and old alike, he must have the courage to develop by himself a Christian culture, a culture which belongs both to the present time and to God, a culture which is therefore a Christian, purified, and exorcized culture. This mission he can fulfil only with the help of courage and light and strength from above. Even so it will happen that this Christian leaven, when mixed with the dough of this world, is fated never to become entirely pure, entirely radiant, entirely aflame. We are still the labourers who must bear the heat and the burden of the day, who will never fully achieve the mission on which we are sent: for the fact remains that this culture, towards which we have a mission and a duty, which we are to perfect in a Christian manner, which we are to continually purify from the power of darkness and of evil, will only reach its fulfilment in the kingdom of God. Before that comes about, we can with the finger of God show signs here and there that the kingdom of God has come into this world in the form of something bright and wholesome, something sound and true. More than this we cannot do. But even this is a noble mission set before us as men and as Christians, a mission against the darkness, to enkindle the faith that the kingdom of God is come.

WE HAVE NOT FAR TO SEEK

Lk 14:16–24; Jn 6:53–56

(Second Sunday after Pentecost)

Today's Gospel tells us the story of the great supper which
God himself has prepared in his Church for those whom
he has invited to the supper of eternal life. Today's text,
therefore, gives us an opportunity to turn our attention
to the mystery of the Eucharist.

It seems to me that out of the immense fullness of
truth and reality of this sacrament there is just one thing
that we should keep in mind—that we receive the body of
Christ. In the course of her doctrinal development the
Church has concentrated her gaze more and more on this
one fact, that Jesus Christ is wholly present in this sacrament,
with his divinity and his humanity, with his flesh and his
blood, with his body and his soul, truly, really, and sub-
stantially present, and that we receive him as the complete
master of our lives to be our food for eternity. This is so
true and so important that, while we may very rightly
follow the mind of the Church in meditating on this
presence, celebrating it, receiving it, praying to it, praising
it, and loving it, it still remains true that the Lord gives
himself to us by granting us, in his own words, his body
as food and his blood as drink. There must be some significance in the fact that the Lord speaks of the presence in

this sacrament, not just of his person but of his body and his blood. If we turn to the discourse promising the Eucharist in the sixth chapter of St John, the discourse which Jesus delivered to his disciples in the synagogue at Capharnaum after the miraculous multiplication of the loaves, we find that it is about his flesh and his blood that he speaks. Jesus here does not use the word "body" which he will use later in the words of institution at the Last Supper; he uses the word "flesh". There is no doubt that this Johannine discourse is meant to refer back to the same word in the prologue of St John's Gospel, where we are told that the Word of God became "flesh". When we ask just why Jesus should give us his body, we should keep in mind this Johannine reference to the flesh in which the Son of Man has come. When John talks about the flesh he means first of all what scripture always means by this word. In Semitic usage it always means the whole man, not just a part of him, not just what we nowadays in an almost medical sense refer to as our body in contradistinction to our spiritual soul. The flesh and the body mean the whole person, but especially the tangible person, that takes its place in this earthly environment, that can be touched, that has a meaningful reality when one touches it and says "This is it," that is not merely spirit and concept and truth and abstract thought, but a concrete human being. Thus John says: "The Word became flesh". By this he means: "Yes, it is here where we are; it is amongst us; it shares our life; it shares space and time; it shares our existence; here we can and must seek the everlasting God." And now Jesus says to us: "Take and eat: this is my body, my flesh." Again and again the earth offers its most desirable possession, the pure and lowly bread and the wine of rejoicing.

From the Last Supper there stretches the unbroken
chain of all those whom Jesus has sent out on his mission
with his word. Link after link falls into place in this succes-
sion of the living bread and the earthly wine, this chain of
human words and human signs. Through these mysterious,
modest, simple proceedings, we receive not merely the
truth of God, not merely or primarily his eternal divinity,
but the flesh and blood of the Son of God, which he eternally took upon himself, from which he shall never be
parted, in which he has immersed himself, so that this
godless world might be filled with the eternal radiance
of the Godhead. So we receive the body and the blood of
the Lord, that body, true, real, earthly, which cost him his
death, that transfigured body which heralds the eternal
transfiguration of the world, to which this body continues
to belong even when it has been transfigured into the life of
God and sits at the right hand of the Father. We need not
seek any further; we have him here where we are; we
can point to him; we can look on him; we can receive him
bodily. And when we are oppressed by the almost overwhelming feeling that we are so far from God, that our
heart is empty of God, when it seems that all the thoughts
and feelings of our heart cannot find him, when we have
the impression that we are here and that God, the true
God, the inaccessible light, the inconceivable, is so far
away—then at least we will want to receive physically
the body of the Lord. It is true that unless the flesh and
blood are received in faith and love they avail us nothing;
they are received for our condemnation. But when we
who are poor and hungry, beggars and cripples, blind and
lame, when we who have been called in from the highways
and hedges of the world, where we thought only to look in
from outside on the splendour of God, when we who are

all too conscious of our poverty and need, of our highway existence, nevertheless enter in as invited guests to this physical banquet of everlasting life, when we can eat the bread of this earth and drink the wine of this land where we live, because we know that it is filled with the eternity of God, when we enter in trustingly and say: "We want to receive even once the body of the Lord", then God must and will make everything different. Then he fills us with his grace and his strength, with his light and his life, even while we think ourselves to be empty and dark, dead and wretched without God. "Take and eat: this is my body". And the Lord says: "He who eats my flesh has eternal life". He has come to us in our flesh and gives us this flesh because we do not know how to come to him. Because he is here, because he himself has come in the flesh of this earth, we want to receive the bread of life, his flesh which is our flesh, and we want to drink the cup of his blood, in which our blood, the blood of our race, has been assumed and eternally redeemed. And because we feel so poor and empty, he gives us what is our own, where we are at home, what we understand, and calls it the pledge of his own divine life.

That is why we can always have confidence in him as our feelings tell us, and enter into this banquet of eternal life, because he is where we are and we have no cause to fear that he is far away; for he has given us his body and blood which are eternal life.

THERE IS SOMETHING MYSTERIOUS
ABOUT THE KINGDOM OF GOD

Lk 14:16–24

(Second Sunday after Pentecost)

Today's Gospel comes from the 14th chapter of St Luke's Gospel, verses 16 to 24. A similar parable is found in St Matthew in the 22nd chapter, verses 1 to 14. Here in St Luke we have the parable of the banquet which a man arranges—so the evangelist tells us—and to which he invites his guests. In the 22nd chapter of St Matthew we have the parable of the royal wedding feast which the king holds for his son and to which he invites his guests. The exegetes ask whether these two texts refer to a single parable told by Jesus or whether he in fact told two different parables with a similar theme. Whichever may be the case, the basic thought in the two parables is the same.

To this royal banquet of eternity, to the kingdom of God, the first people to be invited are those who seem to us to have the right to be invited first, since they have the necessary qualification for such an invitation and will therefore accept the invitation—but in fact they do not accept it. Then others are invited to this royal banquet of eternity, people who seem to us not to possess the qualification that would fit them for this invitation and who should therefore refuse it—and yet we see that they accept it. They become the guests of the house-holder or the king at this feast which—translated into reality—stands for the eternity of blessed fulfilment. In each case there is the basic thought which our Lord seems to be expressing that those who were first invited but refused are the Pharisees, the party of the pious, the orthodox. And those who do not seem to be called and yet accept the invitation are the tax-collectors and the sinners, those who in the estimation of the pious of that time were shut out from the messianic promise, from the covenant which God had made with his chosen people.

When we apply this parable of Jesus to ourselves, then—let us make no bones about it—it can frighten us; for if we accept these two great classes into which Jesus divides men and ask ourselves to which of them we belong, we must answer that we belong to the first-invited. We are Catholics; we are baptized; we belong to the one, true, holy Church; we are to all appearances pious. Now it does not, of course, follow that our history must develop in the same way as today's Gospel. But we must plainly recognize that what is set down here may easily happen to us, because we can be one of the first-invited who made their excuses. And it is true that the kingdom of God does not consist merely in those things which we certainly are: baptized Christians, churchgoers, people who do not come into any open conflict with the Church and her commandments—all this is relevant but it is not identical with the kingdom of God. So we too, who already seem to be inside, are invited to enter truly and to belong to the royal banquet of the true and interior kingdom of God. Here we can really be among those who excuse themselves. The invitation to the kingdom of God and to its royal banquet of eternal life is not something that is given once for all time: it happens again and again that God calls us to obedience to his will, to resignation in the face of his decrees, to self-denial, to his love, to the carrying of the cross, to the unrewarded daily grind, to silence when we want to speak bitter words, to a thousand things which are invitations to the royal banquet and do not seem so. Here the parable breaks down. Here in order to meet the invitation we must remember that it will not of course come in the form of a holy message from the eternal God, nor will someone come to us in great splendour, obviously sent from God, who will expressly inform us in clear and unambiguous terms that this is something that concerns the eternal kingdom of God. No, this happens without pomp or circumstance; this happens in the depths of our conscience, this usually happens almost incidentally. It is then that we may be among those who say: "Hold me excused: I have something else to do."

We have no farm to buy and no oxen to examine and no earthly wedding to celebrate; but when we receive these secret, interior, hidden, obscure, invitations to God in his cross and in his love, we have a thousand other things to do which seem to us much more pressing: business, work, worldly success—I cannot say what it may be, but each one must examine his own heart and he will find enough things there which he uses as excuses with God to avoid accepting his invitation. Where and when this happens, no man can say to another, unless the other bares his conscience in detail and his adviser has a true eye for God's will through the light of God.

But can we not ask ourselves another question, prompted by today's Gospel: can we not ask where and when we make this refusal to God and with such apparently good reason? When we reflect on the text of the Gospel we see that the reasons given seem good ones. Or can a man never miss some meal or other and excuse himself because

he has bought a farm or a pair of oxen or because he is celebrating his own wedding? Jesus has so constructed his story
that one is almost forced to make a charge of unreasonable-
ness against it: Can this householder be angry with these first
invited guests for not coming when they have such important things to do? In other words, applying it to ourselves,
must we be always reminding ourselves of the danger of
using excuses that seem to us good and valid? Is there anyone
who has never said: "I could never stand for that"? In fact he
could but did not want to, and so with these words repro-
duced exactly the sentiment expressed here in the Gospel:
"Hold me excused", meaning that this excuse must be accepted even if it means a refusal to be called deeper into the
mystery of the kingdom of God, for instance through the
silent suffering of injustice. There are a thousand excuses
which have been used by us poor sinners, cowardly and com-
placent earthlings. In this form or that, on this occasion or
that, the kingdom of God passed us by and may well have
found instead those whom we judge to be wicked, impious,
sinful. There is something mysterious about the kingdom
of God. We can only beg God to call us in such a way that
our ears will be opened, that we will hear his call and come.
We can only beg him to give us the strength of a brave
and unselfish heart, so that we will not make excuses that,
in the sight of God and in the pitiless light of his eternity,
are no excuses at all.

In today's prayer we say: "May God grant us a holy fear
and love of his name, since he does not deny his leadership
to those who are grounded in both." If he gives us the pure
and holy fear of rejecting his invitation to us, and the love
that is stronger than all our self-seeking, then he will lead
us to find the right road now and in the future and to attain
to the eternal banquet of living happiness.

PROFITING FROM EVERY SITUATION

Lk 16:1–9

(Eighth Sunday after Pentecost)

Today's Gospel is one we have often read, and probably often wondered about. For it is really strange that Jesus should choose a story like this, drawn from the shabby workaday world, as a parable of the sublime, of his own message, of the kingdom of God that he came to bring us. Here is a rogue—we may as well call a spade a spade—who has been swindling his employer; and when he is about to lose his job because he has been found out, he contrives a master-stroke that will leave him comfortably off for life. Jesus uses this unsavoury story as a parable—an image or comparison—of the way we should act in the kingdom of God. Jesus, the Holy One, infinitely sensitive, who alone was actually able to ask, "Which of you convicts me of sin?", he who alone really knew evil, as we can never know it, regards this earthly, shabby, mean, nasty little affair with perfect detachment, so casually that he can make of it another comparison with the kingdom of heaven.

Be frank. Are there not times when we feel oppressed by the gloom, the meanness, the petty egotism, the spite, the gossip, all the things that make up our routine? Are we not often grieved to find that people are so crude, so unprepared to be understanding; that even good people, who are struggling and praying to become compassionate, fail to understand us, pass coldly by, unmoved by our distress? The world often seems so bitter, so narrow, so heartless, so mean a place. On closer examination, of course, we see that we often grieve over the wretched world when it causes us pain, but much less often when it does not. But however that may be, perhaps we could to some extent imitate Jesus in this matter—even ask him for an attitude very like his own. He has told us that his heavenly Father allows wheat and weeds to grow in the one field which is the world. He was patient and long-suffering, a sober realist—which is why he puts up with us. Must we not imitate him a little and bear with his world—our environment, our fellowmen, our Church—so that God may also bear with us? For if he does not, what is to become of us?

I think there is a second thing we can learn from this parable today. What exactly is the prudence of the dishonest steward which his master praises and which Jesus himself sets before us for our imitation? We might say that he is prudent in contriving to turn every situation to his own advantage. While he was steward he lined his pockets; and now that he is to be dismissed he profits from his new circumstances, though they are the opposite of what he has been accustomed to. As long as he was steward, it would presumably have been disadvantageous for himself to reduce the debts that were owing to his master. Now he seizes the opportunity which could not present itself then. He is prudent because he derives advantage for himself from every situation. That is his prudence. An earthly and vulgar prudence, but the Lord uses it to teach us the heavenly prudence we should have. What does this mean for us?

Our life is a series of vicissitudes. The landscape of the

soul is exposed to every kind of weather. By turns we are happy and unhappy; now lively, now weary; now pleased with our surroundings, now disappointed and hurt; now young, now old; now encouraged by success, now crushed by some bitter failure; now grateful for all the benefits we receive, now wounded by the thought of all that is denied us. Ups and downs, like those of the steward in the Gospel. But are we as prudent as he was? Have we the faith, the stout heart, the humble mind, the docility to God's good pleasure, to see in the most contrasting fortunes of our lives a chance to bring forth fruit for eternity, to prove our love for God, to be patient and courageous, unassuming and devoted; or do we insist on having our own way in the service that we offer God, are we prepared to find him only in the particular situation we have chosen? Before we know it, he has sent us a different situation; and we have not the magnanimity, the willing, loving, uninhibited prudence, to perceive God's call, his work for us, in the different situation, to accept it with a will, to get on with it, to be well-content with God's good pleasure for us. We are not so prudent as the steward in the Gospel. And yet we should be. If the heart is really kept open and ready for God, anything that may happen to us in life can be accepted as a grace and a blessing. Of course this means having a heart that is well disposed and humble, that listens and obeys. But why not ask God for that gift? Could we not pray instead of complaining, call on God instead of accusing others? Somewhere in the life of every human being is a wound that has never healed. For we should be saints in the literal sense of the word—holy people—if always and in all things we were at one with God and his will. It is because we are not, that the parable of the Christian's heavenly prudence concerns us all. If we will only look a little more closely at our lives, we shall find situations, relationships, burdens, here and there, that can only be seen for what they are, can only be coped with, if we are prudent enough by God's grace to acknowledge with a heavenly prudence: This too is a word of God's eternal love; I must be loving and courageous and answer yes.

ONE SMALL CANDLE IN THE DARKNESS

Luk 18: 31–43

(Quinquagesima)

Today's Gospel is at once stern and consoling. It has two parts, with no direct connexion between them. The first part contains the third prophecy of the Lord's passion, and the second part the miracle worked for the blind man outside Jericho.

This third prophecy of the passion, which occurs here in the 18th chapter of St Luke, is also found in Matthew, chapter 20 and Mark, chapter 10. But if we compare the Lucan text with Matthew and Mark, one thing strikes us. Though the three accounts agree almost word for word, Luke stresses the fact that the disciples do not understand the prophecy. Now I think we might meditate a little on this point.

Those who we are plainly told did not understand the words of Christ—which we find so easy to understand—are none others than the Twelve, his apostles, the foundation stones of his Church, Peter and the other eleven, whom he chose, whom he called, who saw his miracles, whom he gathered about him so as to make them the beginning of the new people of God. They do not understand what he is saying. They cannot grasp the fact that he must suffer. They are not even willing to make head or tail of his declaration that in three days he will rise again. The evangelist uses three expressions to tell us that they understand nothing. If we translate quite literally, then we may render them as follows: The disciples cannot take in any of what is said, and the saying is hidden from them. They can make nothing, they are unwilling to make head or tail, of what they are told. In the first place we are simply given the fact: they cannot take in what is said, they cannot fit it into what they already know, they cannot draw this darkness into the light that illumines their lives. Then in the second place the matter is obscure in objective reality; it is said in extenuation that this saying is something hidden, wrapped in the darkness of mystery, so that it is not accessible to the disciples. But however that may be, we are told in the third place that they make no real effort to penetrate the mystery which confronts them, no real effort to understand it.

This is said of apostles, and it is said of them three times. Yet we must add that the apostles remain with Jesus. Even when they see that they do not understand what is going on, they remain steadfast. They are faithful. They are patient. They make Jesus, as it were, an advance payment of confidence and time, giving him a chance to grow in their hearts. And we must add that God bears with them. Though their hearts are darkened, though they do not understand, though in their inertia they hardly want to understand, they remain undergirt by God's mercy, his faithfulness, his providence, and his love. Mystery uncomprehended stands between them and the Lord, yet does not separate them. Neither abandons the other. Each cleaves to the other, because God loves and is faithful, because man realizes that though he may not understand the mystery, God and God's loyal grace are only to be found where that mystery is.

Is there a lesson here for our own life? If we compare all that we can grasp and understand, all that is clear and straightforward in our lives, with the obscure and the baffling, the hidden and uncomprehended, the mysterious and unspeakable, then we seem to see a tiny candle burning in the midst of endless darkness. How can it be otherwise so long as we are here making our way among parabolic shadows, still on pilgrimage towards the everlasting light, the unapproachable light that only God can be?

Would it not be folly to expect everything to be intelligible, or to accept no more than we can understand? The incomprehensible must lay hold on us, for only then shall we be open to God the infinite, and only if we are that, have we the hope and the promise that we shall find everything.

Let us be patient and faithful. Let us wait, and accept the incomprehensible from God's hand. Let us believe, even when God tells us truths through his Gospel and through his providential dispensation—that is, when he tells us what he wishes to through what we do not understand.

The same word, the same Greek word, used here in Luke, chapter 18, is used of a woman in chapter 2. She did not understand the saying which he spoke to her, and it is written of her that she kept all these things in her heart. Let us faithfully keep what we do not understand in our own heart. One day the infinite light of beatitude will burst forth from it.

A VOICE IN THE WILDERNESS

Jn 1:19–28

(Third Sunday in Advent)

After the prologue, the general introduction, and the summing up, St John opens his Gospel with a portrait of St John the Baptist. Plainly, he is thought of as an Advent figure, the representative human being midway between the past and the coming of the Lord. No wonder, then, that the Church conjures up the figure of the Baptist in two of her Advent Gospels, in order to tell us what Advent is. For the Lord has come and yet he is still coming. He is already here, but is in our midst, still, as the hidden God; and so we are still men who have no lasting city here, pilgrims between time and eternity, men who must still await God's coming, men who keep Advent even at Christmastime and must remember that we are still at the beginnings, still on pilgrimage; that we must still make our way through time, amid sorrow and distress, but with a heart full of faith, towards the eternal light that still awaits us. What this means for us is that eternity is not yet here. But it does not mean that we must not cherish the light that is already lit, and it does not mean that we ought to turn our backs upon this world. It means that we must not neglect the other light. We should look to the Precursor.

He is in the wilderness. Obviously because he finds these

surroundings appropriate to his life—the parched solitude, the endless spaces, where no one can feel at home. Inevitably we keep discovering that we too are in the wilderness, the wilderness of a great city, the wilderness of isolation, a wilderness that seems to have no centre, a wilderness we cannot feel at home in. And we are also men who would live in a wilderness if we had to give our outward environment the shape of that which is within us.

Then scripture says that the emissaries of the Pharisees ask John who he is, indeed half suggest that he has only to seize his opportunity and his whole life will come to fruition. Why not? The Lord himself has said that among those born of women none is greater than John. But John says: "No, I am not." Do we not experience something similar in our own lives? Have we not constantly to take a firm stand and say: No, I am not —I am not strong, I am not blessed, I am not one who has a happy life ahead of him. Time and again a man is put to the test, to see whether he will hold his ground and say no; for the real meaning of my life consists in admitting my pettiness and sinfulness, so as to clear a space and allow meaning to enter my life. Somehow or other we too must be people who renounce self-assertion and our towering pride, to say: I am not. All I am, says the Precursor, is the voice of one crying in the wilderness.

How strange! This is a quotation from Isaiah, and here is the voice from the wilderness where everything is swallowed up by the wind, where nothing has any settled shape, where the cry is lost upon the air. Dies away, that is, but is not lost. For though it reaches nothing else, it does reach the One to whom it is addressed. And so it always means something other than itself. We too should be the voice of one crying in the wilderness, should cry to God continually although our cry seems to be swallowed up by the endless silence and solitude, and even when there seems to be no answer to our call. We shall hear the answer. It is not just an echo, not simply consolation in the faith; it is the eternal word of God himself, filling this emptiness—the wilderness of my heart that is so often left waiting without hope and without faith, in the desolation of this life—filling it with eternal light, eternal truth, the eternal reality that is the only reality.

But we must not say these three things and leave it at that. There is a fourth thing to be said: Among you stands one who is to come, the unknown one and the long awaited, as we best know him. And because the invisible is something we cannot do without—for it is the ultimate bond between alpha and omega—it is true that he is already in our midst: in all our wildernesses, in every feeble self-denial, in every whispered cry to him, he is already here.

Yet it is always Advent in this Christmastide. What a harsh Gospel! We shall only find consolation in it if God gives us the grace to do so. All the same shall we not hold out a little while in the wilderness of our life? Even if we must always be saying no. Even if we must keep taking leave of ourselves, keep tasting the bitterness of our desolate world. Even then shall we not say to the unshakable centre of our lives: You are here. You are the Lord of my faith, you are my strength and my delight. You are the Christmas in the Advent of my existence?

TECHNOLOGY MULTIPLIES THE LOAVES

Jn 6: 1–15

(Fourth Sunday in Lent)

What happens in the Gospel that is read to us today?
We hear of people driven on by a hunger for God. They
follow Jesus into the wilderness. They follow him there
because they realize that their own life is a wilderness,
because at the bottom of their hearts they know that man
needs God and God's word. They are looking for a prophet,
they hunger for God's word, they demand more than their
ordinary life is able to offer them. So they go; they go
into the wilderness; they leave the places where they
have their homes and the bread of their earthly existence.
And strange to say, while they are hungering this way for
God, an earthly hunger seizes them. While they are looking
for God, they perceive that they are men, who must have
their earthly bread, who must try to defend their earthly
existence. Hungering for God, they find themselves
hungering for earthly life. The situation becomes still
stranger: the man that they are following, so that he may
break the bread of eternity for them, the man from whom
they expected nothing but the words of eternal life, gives
them earthly bread, looks after their earthly existence,
fears that they may perish in the wilderness. Stranger and
stranger, they halt and sit down, they are fed, their hunger is

satisfied, and in verse 26 of this chapter Jesus tells us what happens next. "Truly, truly," he says, "I say to you, you seek me, not because you saw signs, but because you ate your fill of the loaves." At the end of today's Gospel, chapter 6, verse 14, we read: "When the people saw the sign that he had done, they said, 'This is indeed the prophet who is to come into the world!'" And so they want to make him their king. Because they sought the bread of eternity, God also gives them the bread of this world; and because he gives it to them, they begin to lose interest in him and his eternal life and to seek earthly bread once more. They want to make their God the king of their earthly life. When they have eaten their fill, they are more eager than ever for the bread of this life; and what was only meant to give them leasure and freedom of mind for seeking God, becomes a temptation, tempts them to covet earthly well-being and the joys of earthly life and even to pervert the gift of God.

And then, we are told, Jesus withdrew into the hills by himself. Because they were that way, because they perverted God's gift, because eating their fill only made them the hungries for the things of this world, God, who had given them even their earthly bread, withdrew from them. Now this is only a parable of what constantly happens in the life of mankind and of the individual, particularly in our technological age. God gives us technology in order that we may have our earthly bread and be able to multiply it so as to feed the great multitude in the wilderness of this world. This miracle, whereby technology multiplies the loaves, is granted us so that we may have time to desire God's bread and satisfy our hunger for eternity. And we, like the people in that other wilderness, are tempted by the miracle to want still more and to make God king of our technology.

But he withdraws from us. He stays by himself on the mountain of his eternity and will not lend himself to our scheme. And once again we find ourselves alone, in a still more savage wilderness despite the twelve baskets of miraculous bread with which we are still encumbered.

Let us not say that technology, civilization, a rising standard of living, comfort, the wider scope that is opening up for our earthly existence, presents no special temptation to us personally. We may not be the most self-indulgent people of our age; perhaps we have not really had our fair share of the bread that technology passes on to us from God. But we are the very people who are tempted, and who (perhaps without committing any discernible sin) often succumb to the temptation. Is there not something to the quip that people can be divided into two classes, those who have a car and those who wish they had one? Are we not often the ones who covet things, who remain inwardly dissatisfied even though we really have enough of the bread of this life and ought to desire God more? Have we often given up earthly things that we could have, simply to show God that we love him? Do we not condemn this demonic technological world only when we must do without something that we covet in our heart of hearts? Do we modern Christians live considerably below the heights, or even in the very abyss of this age, because we are incapable of anything better? Have we the clarity of mind and the stout heart to develop a soundly Christian pattern of life, in the midst of a technological age that we affirm and accept as our lot—one that will uphold the right scale of values not only in theory but also in day to day reality? Or must Christ say to us too: You do not follow me because you recognize your age as a token of

God's goodness, but because you have stuffed yourselves with bread and want still more?

Ah, today's Gospel has much to teach us about our age, about our intimate selves, if we will only face our life and take its true measure: life in the age of technology, which as a whole, if not in every detail, is willed by God because he means it to multiply the loaves. Otherwise, though nothing is said about this in our hymn-books, we too may become involved in a mysterious way in the sinfulness of our age. Everyone contributes something to the spirit of the age. And everyone is called upon to live in such a way, for his own part, that his age may be one when God can rely on our clarity of mind, on the love of our hearts for him, and give us the bread of this world, so that in the wilderness of this life we may receive the bread of everlasting life for eternity.

TAKEN UP IN THE
ETERNAL DAY OF THE SON

Jn 8:46–59

(Passion Sunday)

Today's Gospel contains part of the controversies that Jesus carried on in the temple during his sojourn in Jerusalem for the feast of tabernacles. We might consider it under two headings: What does Jesus say about himself? And what conception of himself, according to St John, does Jesus reveal here?

The first thing that Jesus says is that he comes from God. He exists from all eternity. "Truly, truly," he says, "before Abraham was, I am." He is speaking with his human words, and therefore what he says he is thinking with his human thoughts, with his human soul, with his created mind which did not always exist, which came into being when he was conceived by the doing of God in the womb of the Blessed Virgin. Yet he knows that he is the one who dwells with the Father from all eternity, who appears and speaks and acts with this created reality which is his human nature. If one may put it that way, he feels it in his bones: I who stand here, I who speak, I who appear, I am the one who is with the Father from all eternity. Here speaks an I—that is, a person—who is God himself. And so this day that he speaks of includes all the days which make up the history of finitude, and at heart everybody must rejoice to see the dawning of Christ's day, the one day of eternity, which shall have no evening.

In the second place, Jesus says that he tells the truth. He says, "If I did not speak as I do, I should be a liar like you". By this he does not mean that men often tell untruths. If he calls poor human creatures liars, he means something more. He is thinking of all that is brittle, fragmentary, obscure, discordant, and opaque in our souls; and then he perceives that he is different from other men, that he is at one with himself, knows what he is and what he wants, perfectly understands himself, is not darkness as we are, we who creep painfully from one shattering experience of ourselves to the next, experiences that at once belie and unmask us, laying bare all the fatal flaws, all the black abysses there within. This Son of Man who comes from God knows he is not like that, he behind whose human nature stretches the seamless eternity of God; he knows that he is not like other men. He tells the truth, he is truth.

And in the third place, as Jesus says, he does not seek his own glory; he obediently serves the Father and does his will. Though Jesus is nothing less than the revelation of God in this world, though he is the existence and the presence of God on earth, though he is the self-disclosure of the eternal God among us, he does not seek his own glory but the will of him who sent him, the will of him from whom he proceeds as the Son, the Word, from all eternity; and he would save us, he would rescue us, he would bring us God's mercy. And so he who is before Abraham was, is also selflessness, defencelessness, service, devotion, self-effacement, sheer mercy incarnate. He is the one who can only think of himself in terms of something quite other—the Father, or his own being-in-us. He is the true middle, which only exists because it proceeds from one thing and connects it with another, the Mediator in all his fulness and human reality. He is the Word which the Father utters for us as well as for himself, the salvation which is only where it wants to be, if it has reached us and taken root in our hearts as that self-revealing Word of the Father.

In the fourth place, therefore, Jesus knows that he is the sinless one. "Which of you convicts me of sin?", he asks. He asks this question in the infinite humility of his human heart, without self-assertion, without boasting; he cannot help seeing himself for what he is, experiencing himself just as he is made in his created humanity, just as he is begotten in his eternal generation by the Father—the unalloyed expression of the eternal, holy Father. And so: Who can accuse me of sin? He knows that he is pure service, pure devotion, pure obedience, pure love, God's sheer prodigality to the world; and he knows that all this is the diametric opposite of all that we must call sin—self-isolation, self-assertion, refusal to serve, refusal to devote oneself, trying to keep oneself for oneself, refusal to listen, indocility to God: all that is sin, and all that is the utter opposite of what Jesus knows, experiences, and declares himself to be in this text. And we shall have to say that we are also the opposite of what he is. But no: we may, and must, say something different. We are sons in the Son, God's beloved children, because he is the one who speaks to us today. So we may and must say: We are the ones God has thought of from all eternity, we are truly caught up in the Son's eternal day. In that day we are thought of, in that day we are loved, in that day we are foreseen, in that day we are preserved, by the faithfulness of the everlasting God. We are the ones, too, who come from God and his love. And so we must not seek our own glory but God's service. We are the ones who daily experience God's word anew: Your sins are forgiven, you are sanctified, justified, loved; God's Holy Spirit has been given to you to be the centre of your life and your love; shaken by God's forgiving grace in his Son, you, a child of God, may say with St Paul to the darkness of this world: He has delivered me from the dominion of darkness and transferred me to the kingdom of his beloved Son. So by God's grace we have a self-awareness that constantly asserts itself, by God's grace, against that other, native one we have as stiffnecked sinners, as lying human beings. In the ultimacy of that light we simply believe and flee to the Son who speaks to us like this today as to our salvation and Redeemer, our grace and justification.

And when we do so, we can say something more about ourselves than our mere human, earthly experience of ourselves would have us say. If we are children of the Father, sons in the Son, then the glory that the Son tells us today is his, is destined for us as well, now and forever.

NATURE ABHORS A VACUUM

Jn 16: 5–14

(Fourth Sunday after Easter)

Today's Gospel is taken from the words of the Lord at
the Last Supper, as given in Jn 16:5–14. Jesus speaks of
the future, he takes his leave of the apostles and consoles
them. It is difficult to deal with this text in order because
in a very deep and authentic sense Jesus keeps saying the
same thing—all there is to say. We might say that the
fourteenth chapter has to do with consoling the apostles
over Jesus's departure and with the promise of the Spirit;
and chapters 15 and 16 might be summed up in his words:
Abide in me, and I in you. Chapter 17 can be called Christ's
high priestly prayer. Again we might say that chapters
15 and 16 comprise two parts: the first, chapter 15, could
be entitled: the fellowship and destiny of the disciples;
and the second, chapter 16, consolation of the disciples in the
Holy Ghost and in the prospect of soon seeing Christ
again. Today's text belongs to this latter part. We might
also entitle the first fifteen verses of chapter 16: the Holy
Ghost and his work. For from verse 4 onwards Jesus says
something about the relationship of the Holy Ghost with
the world, and in the following verses something about
the relationship of the Holy Ghost with the disciples of
Jesus. Let us briefly consider these verses together and

see whether they may not bring a little light and consolation and seriousness into our lives.

Jesus is speaking of his departure. He says that he must go and that of all this mysterious process whereby Jesus dies, seems to leave the world, and returns to his Father, the disciples understand only the absence of their Lord, only the emptiness compared with the presence he has been to them. Only distance and separation. That is why sorrow has filled their hearts. Do we not have this experience of parting, time and again; of some person or some thing that is dear to us leaving us, taking our very selves away? Our heart is filled with sorrow; we are threatened with the grief of this world that knows no hope and that kills a deadly grief. Because I have said these things to you, sorrow has filled your hearts, says the Lord. He does not blame them so much for this as for not asking where he is going, for not asking him to tell them the true nature of this going. My going, Jesus tells his disciples, is the coming of the Father and existence in the Holy Ghost. We must not take this superficially, as though Jesus simply said, Yes I am going, but to console you I shall send you the Holy Ghost. He does do this, but we shall only understand the passage if we apprehend—at least by faith—that, as the Lord says here, his going actually is the coming of God's Spirit. We might put it this way: There is no such thing, either in the world or in the heart, as literal vacancy, as a vacuum. And wherever space is really left by parting, by death, by renunciation, by apparent emptiness, provided the emptiness that cannot remain such is not filled by the world, or activity, or chatter, or the deadly grief of the world—there God is. When he is in the heart in this way we call him the Holy Spirit, because he is revealed to us out of the fulness of the Godhead, by the mercy of the

Father, and sent to us as the Spirit of the Son. If Jesus takes from us what seems to us his palpable presence, what we in our folly think of as his only real palpable presence, takes from us the consolation of the utterable and the tangible, of what can be seen and possessed, then, if we believe in him, he comes to us in the Holy Ghost. That is why he says: "It is to your advantage that I go away; for if I go, I will send the Spirit to you." But the Spirit cannot come into hearts that will not open themselves to this awful emptiness, as it seems to be, which is filled by the Spirit of God; hearts that are unbelieving, that are the "world" in the sense meant here. What happens in such hearts shows us the negative counterpart of the Spirit's dominion. When he comes, Jesus says, he will convince the world of sin and of righteousness and of judgement. How does the Spirit do that? By this sinful sorrow—even if he protests against it—man knows in his heart that he is not in the truth, not in righteousness, but in sin. He perceives his sin because he does not believe in Jesus who is given in the Spirit. The despairing emptiness within tells man that somebody has gone and that true righteousness exists when one loves the world enough to reach out, unafraid, beyond the world, has the courage to leave oneself open to the unutterable, when one believes that one possesses everything although one seems to have lost everything, that one has conquered although in this going of Christ one seems to have been defeated. And so the emptiness that is deadly because it is not filled by the Spirit of God convinces the world that the only righteousness consists in acknowledging that the Son goes to the Father and is no more seen; that no man is right who does not accept this fact. By this darkness which will not allow itself to be illumined by that unutterable light, the prince of this world is already judged. For the judgement is that the man who does not abandon himself to trusting faith has already judged himself in this deadly emptiness, in this despairing darkness. But with you, my disciples, Jesus says, the case is different: the Spirit comes ever anew, ever more abundantly, in this experience that seems so dark. When Jesus seems to have nothing more to say to us, then he is telling us what he wished to tell us but was not able to when he was tangibly present—the secret of his death, which is life; of our death, which is eternal life. That is why he says: "I have yet many things to say to you, but you cannot bear them now." But when the Spirit of truth has come—that is, I who now take leave of you—, then I shall lead you not into this or that partial truth, but into all truth. For the Spirit does not speak of something or other; he speaks of me who have entered with your own destiny into my Father's infinity. He declares what he hears—ultimately, what he is—, the eternal wisdom of God himself which blossoms in silence, in the experience of our own crucifying finitude. He will not speak on his own authority, Jesus says, but whatever he hears he will speak, and he will declare to you the things that are to come—God himself. He will glorify me, for he will take what is mine and declare it to you.

We are always approaching the ascension of Jesus, and it always seems to us to be a parting. This thing that happened to Jesus keeps happening in our own lives. As we pilgrims journey on towards the parting, let us look squarely at it. So long as we believe, and accept what we undergo as the lot of the Lord and his disciples, the Holy Ghost will always come with his life, with his righteousness, with all truth, and lead us into God's eternal life and light.

THE SPIRIT OF
TRUTH ACCUSES THE WORLD!

Jn 16:5–14

(Fourth Sunday after Easter)

Today's Gospel is taken from St John, chapter 16, from Jesus's farewell to his disciples at the Last Supper. Verses 5–16 of this chapter form a unity which we might entitle: The Paraclete, the Spirit of truth accuses the world and instructs the disciples; for it deals with these two subjects. Let us consider the first part, because it is rather difficult to understand even from a textual point of view. May God give us the grace to understand the holy Gospel a little better and let it speak to us.

First Jesus observes—this is how our passage begins—that the disciples are sorrowful because he has said that he is going away. But in their sorrow, he says, they do not ask where he is going. If they understood that he who has come to redeem the world is returning to the Father, that his going, his death, his loss to them is acceptance by the Father, entering into his glory, the triumph of his redemptive work, then—Jesus says—their heart would no longer be filled with this earthly, wild, despairing sorrow; but they would realize that it must be so, and that by departing from them and returning home he is only the closer to them in his Spirit, who brings the Lord the nearer to the disciples, is going to do: he will judge the world and lead the disciples into all truth, even such truth as they do not yet understand.

St John pictures a trial conducted before the tribunal of God—the trial of the world by the Paraclete, God's Consoler and Advocate, the Spirit of truth. This trial will not await the end of time; it begins now, because the Spirit of God, set free by the death of Jesus, is at work in the world through the pneumatic preaching of Jesus's witnesses.

Jesus says that if the Spirit does not convert the world to the disciples' preaching, at least he will convince it to the extent of showing it what it is in three respects: in respect of sin, of righteousness, and of judgement. There we are, and Jesus explains what these three things mean. He will convince the world of sin: because, the Lord says, it does not believe in me. The term of sin then is always unbelief, failure to believe in him who departed in the weakness of the cross and precisely so enters his home, returns to his Father, precisely so bestows the Spirit through his heart, perforated by the sins of the world. We really must examine our sins to see whether they are not a denial that Jesus has gone to the Father. It is a sin, Jesus says, not to believe me who have gone to the Father through the shame and humiliation of death on the cross. Whenever we sin, we flee the cross of the Lord, we do not believe in his going to the Father. And whenever we do not understand that truth, we are sinners. Now the Spirit is meant to teach us, to convince us who would not accept the scandal of the cross—not in our own lives, not in the Church, not in the world—, that the Holy Spirit of God, of truth, of power, of love, comes in the cross, and that any other opinion is a sin, is a refusal to believe in the crucified and risen Lord who has returned to his Father.

Moreover, Jesus says, the Spirit convinces the world of

righteousness—convinces it that Jesus is right at this trial which is universal history, where the world and the Crucified stand together before the tribunal of the Father, each accusing the other. The righteousness we speak of here is being right, is the very triumph of Jesus at this trial, before this tribunal of world history. The Spirit convinces the world of righteousness: because I am going to the Father, because I am the one whom the Father accepts in death, because I am the one—Jesus means—who having placed his soul in the Father's hands through this frightful death, truly reaches him in what seems to be the moment of defeat, of ruin and disaster. Wherever the folly of the cross is, there he goes to the Father, he is accepted even though we no longer see him, and there he is right. That is what the Spirit convinces the world of: of his being right, of his righteousness.

And thirdly, he convinces the world of judgement, because the prince of this world, Jesus says, is already judged. In Christ's return home redemption is complete, the powers of darkness are stripped of all their real power, the world and all the world rules is already judged. Perhaps this discourse of Jesus's seems remote and abstract to us. But if we examine our own lives, our sorrow, our dissatisfaction, our scepticism, all that our heart may be full of, then I think we can well reread these few verses and by God's grace they may touch our hearts. Then Jesus would say: You are sorrowful because I who am the nearness of your God seem to withdraw into the shadow of death, into infinite distance, because you think I have gone away. But I have gone home, and only so can the Spirit dwell with you, he who can convince you too that not believing in this truth of my going to the Father is the ultimate basis of your sins, and that my going, my being right pronounces judgement even in this world upon the powers of sin that would hold you captive. Believe. Call on the Spirit, call on grace, and the Lord is with you, the Lord who forgives and delivers, frees and sanctifies, and amid the darkness of this world sets up his everlasting kingdom in your heart.

GOD IN YOU DESIRES GOD FOR YOU

Jn 16:23–30

(Fifth Sunday after Easter)

Let us try to meditate on an idea in today's Gospel which is particularly brought out in the first verses but really pervades the whole—the idea of praying for things in Jesus's name.

Jesus tells us to ask for things in his name; he says that such prayer will be heard, that the Father even anticipates it because he knows—if we make our petition in Jesus's name—that it is a prayer of love for him and of faith. Jesus says: If we are heard because we pray this way in his name, then our joy will be full. Petition in Jesus's name. If we do not hastily assume that petition must mean explicitly praying to God in words, explicitly thinking of him, but consider what we are like in our ordinary lives, in our secret moments, we shall see that we are all desire and longing, ever on the lookout for something new and different, that we are a hunger and a thirst for the good things of life, one cry for a fulfilment we do not yet possess. These desires, which are almost identical with ourselves, which we live and are, reach out here, there, and everywhere. It is strange. They contradict each other; they seek the noble and the sublime, and the most concrete of earthly things; they seize us by turns, the longing, the crying out, the yearning, the desires, the wishes, the hungers, begging and imploring. Now it is one thing, now another; we are practically one vast chaos of appetites. There is no help for it, even if we want to be orderly and lucid, well co-ordinated and balanced; we can be nothing else but a multiplicity of desires, and they simply do not, of themselves, present any clear outline, they have no inner cohesion, they are not one harmonious whole in which we could find ourselves and perfect fulfilment. We need someone to straighten out the tangled desires that we are, to infuse them with tranquility and an inner light and joy. Once everything within us is well-ordered, peaceful and coherent, we are a petition, a desire, that *can* be heard. For how can our prayer be answered unless our desire, however manifold, is concentrated on one thing? That is why we must ask in Jesus's name; which does not mean that we invoke him verbally and then desire whatever our turbulent, divided heart or our appetite, our wretched mania for everything and anything, happens to hanker for. No, asking in Jesus's name means entering into him, living by him, being one with him in love and faith. If he is in us in faith, in love, in grace, in his Spirit, and then our petition arises from the centre of our being, which is himself, and if all our petition and desire is gathered up and fused in him and his Spirit, then the Father hears us. Then our petition becomes simple and straightforward, harmonious, sober, and unpretentious. Then what St Paul says in the letter to the Romans applies to us: We do not know how to pray as we ought, but the Spirit himself intercedes for us, praying the one prayer, "Abba! Father!" He longs for that from which the Spirit and Jesus himself have proceeded: he longs for God, he asks God for God, on our behalf he asks for God. Every-

thing is included and contained in this prayer. Not as
though we must not ask him for everything that will in
any way ease, clarify, or illuminate our lives; not as though
we must not ask for our daily bread, and appeal to the
eternal Father in our daily necessities and pain. These
things we should do. But it should all be caught up into
the one great prayer of Christ's Spirit, in the name of
Jesus. Then we shall see that God really answers our
prayer, in one way or another. Then we shall no longer
feel that this "one way or another" is a feeble excuse
offered by the pious, and the Gospel, for unanswered
prayer. No. Our prayer is answered, but precisely because
it is prayer in Jesus's name; and what we ultimately pray
for is for the Lord to grow in our lives, to fill our existence
with himself, to triumph, to gather into one our scattered
life, the thousand and one desires of which we are made.

He answers our prayer, for he gives us himself. Of
course we must accept the gift and not clutch at a thousand
other things. If we reach for the gift—we have Jesus's
word for it—God gives us everything else that we really
need besides. He makes our clamant poverty wealth and
abundances once more. We have only two alternatives:
either to ask the Father in Jesus's name for the good
Spirit—as Jesus says in St Luke—or to be a confusion
of centrifugal desires which divide our heart, rend our life
asunder, and finally run down in death. But to pray in
Jesus's name is to have one's prayer answered, to receive
God and God's blessing; and then, even amid tears, even
in pain, even in indigence, even when it seems that one
has still not been heard, the heart rests in God, and
that—while we are still here on pilgrimage, far from the
Lord—is perfect joy. Always Jesus can say to us: Hitherto
you have asked nothing in my name. You have tried to,

you have meant to, you have started to. But you see, I who gather everything together and reduce everything to one even in your life, I must become the strength and the burden of your prayer, its blessing and its answer. Ask now in my name, as you pray with me the prayer I said on the cross: "Father, into thy hands I commend my spirit"; when I knew that I was returning home to the Father and that on my homecoming he will pour forth the Spirit in your heart, God in you to ask for God for you so that your prayer may be answered and your joy may be full.

THERE STANDS TRUTH

Jn 18:33–37

(Feast of Christ the King)

Today we celebrate the feast of Christ the King, the sovereignty that belongs to Christ, the God-Man, over every created thing, over man and his history, and especially over the human heart.

When we read today's Gospel, which is taken from the passion, it strikes us as an odd choice for this feast. Christ stands there before a proconsul of the Roman Empire, a ruler of this world, accused by both the religious and the political authorities of his nation, and is condemned to death. Scourged and crowned with thorns, he stands there, and Pilate says with a gesture of pity but full of disgust: Here is the man. And the man whose servants do not fight for him, who is handed over to a pagan power, is presented to us as our king. And when he announces the kingship with which today's Gospel has to do, he says to us: "Yes, I am a king. For this I was born, and for this I have come into the world, to bear witness to the truth. Every one who is of the truth hears my voice."

Of course his kingship embraces more than we are told of in today's Gospel. But Jesus is king precisely because he has come to bear witness to the truth. What truth is meant here? We can only understand the verse if we realize exactly what St John understands by truth. This

Johannine truth has no plural, and is not the same thing as truth in the sense of a set of propositions. It means the antithesis of the world: For this I was born and have come into the world. What is this world in St John? Here we must be precise. It is not the world which provides a house for our life, which we like, where we feel at ease. The world in St John is something different, whatever it may mean in other contexts. For him the world is darkness which shuts God out, which will not receive the light. The world is what is dying, what is perishing; the world is sin, anguish, and judgement. Johannine truth is the antithesis of all this. It is the thing that is one, wholly compact, unchanging, reliable, the thing that comes from God, that he must disclose, whose coming still has a history in this dark world, that is only there if God reveals it. Truth with John is one of those ideas, like light and life, that say everything and embrace everything which is our salvation, which comes from God, which he reveals, which is only there if he takes us into this reality. So John says in chapter 17 that the devil is not in the truth. We do not have the truth, we are in it. That is why verse 37 says that every one who is of the truth hears his word. It is this truth we are dealing with here, this deed of God, this revealed reality. And Jesus says: Because I bear witness to this truth I am the king of this world. Now to understand this saying we must bear in mind Jesus's conviction that he himself is this truth that has come into the world. Because he is there, because the Son—his quintessence—is there, because his sinlessness has appeared, because his love has revealed itself even unto the cross, therefore God's truth is there and bears witness to itself. He is king because he is this truth, brings it to us, attests it; because this divine truth undergoes that fate in the world which we read of here in the Gospel. The self-revealing truth of God's faithfulness, of his saving mercy, stands there in the person of Jesus: accused, scourged, crowned with thorns, soon to be pierced by the lance of this world. There is God's truth and his reality, exposing itself to such a fate, bearing triumphant witness to itself by submitting to the ignoring which the lying world holds in store for it. We say we are university people and deal with truth, and we inscribe our buildings with the text: "The truth shall make you free." If we do not understand this truth, this kingship of Christ, we may be clever, we may be scholars, but we are not in the truth which alone is light and salvation, life and eternity. We must understand this truth of the cross, this self-abasement unto death, if we would understand anything about truth and not just about the theses of the learned. And we must also bear witness to this truth by what we sacrifice and what we venture. We must want to be witnesses of Christ and subjects of his kingdom, and have the courage to accept abasement. Right and truth are not necessarily what seems noble and glorious, what the world will accept and heartily applaud. No, the light shines in the darkness and the darkness has not comprehended it. In us too there is that darkness. That shrinking from the light is part of our own heart, and so Jesus the man of sorrows stands before us and says to us: "Every one who is of the truth hears my voice." Without making pronouncements about the Church and her power, without thinking of the Church in terms of party politics, could we not make room in our hearts and say: Disperse the darkness of my heart and allow your truth—which is humility, faithfulness, hoping against hope, blessed truth—to be in me, so that your power may triumph by drawing everything to you, as you hang there, lifted up upon the cross—even my poor heart.

A UNIVERSE MADE TO OUR MEASURE

Rom 8:18–23

(Fourth Sunday after Pentecost)

The letter to the Romans is the longest and most pregnant of the apostolic letters in the New Testament, and the eighth chapter, which contains today's text, is the climax of that letter. St Paul devotes his first eight chapters to showing that man is not justified and sanctified by his own efforts, by independently fulfilling the law of God, but by God's grace. Grace must precede anything man does in that order, it is in no way due to man, it is given him by the sheer goodness and benignity of God; it and God's Holy Spirit—on whom one lays hold by believing in this gracious, unmerited doing of God—make man holy and just, snatch him from the dark powers of this world, give him the victory over them, enable him to look confidently towards his future. This is what St Paul is saying here, once he has shown the sinfulness of all mankind and its need of redemption; once he has said that this justice which comes not from men but from God, must be steeped in faith, and transforms a man. Now chapter 8 describes this justice.

It is approached from two points of view: Paul tells us what man now is through the spirit of sonship that is poured forth in his heart; and he tells us where man, thus justified, is going. Inasmuch as man is now a child of God, he is already a new creature. Inasmuch as he has just begun his course, is journeying towards the true fulfilment of what he already is, man remains subject to the premessianic age; he is in transition. The past and the future meet within the framework of his existence. He finds himself as it were on a bridge, crossing over from this sinful life that is forfeit to death and the law, into God's freedom. That is why he is still exposed to the sufferings of this world, why he still groans with this age, this world, that is subject to corruption. But he knows that that is entirely provisional and transitory, that it will all be done away with; and so Paul says: "I consider that the sufferings of this present time are not worth comparing with the glory that is to be revealed in us." It is a glory which we already possess in germ in the Spirit of God, a glory which has only to be revealed in due course, which must burst forth from the centre of our existence, seize upon every sphere, every dimension of our earthly being, and transform it, subject it to this higher law of God, this glory of God. And so what we have still to suffer in this passing age is not to be compared with the glory that is to come, that is to be revealed in us.

Now Paul turns from the individual Christian. What he suffers, after all, is only a share in the nature of existence, in the destiny of the world as a whole. Because we are earthly, fleshly men, because we are still subject to this our time, to this aeon, we must suffer. Sickness and death are not simply forces that murderously fall upon us with one accord. According to St Paul, they are dark, cosmic powers, ultimately the spawn of sin, at work everywhere in the world. In the whole of nature St Paul sees this darkness at work, affecting us individuals almost incidentally. So he goes on to say: "For the creation waits with eager longing for the revealing of the sons of God." We men of today see things quite differently. We feel that we have been thrust into a world that is alien to us, alien to man and his lot. But Paul sees the world in the light of God, which means that he sees it in relation to the one Creator of heaven and earth, of all things visible and invisible, of all time and of every age. And since he sees the world in relation to its single origin, he recognizes that it has been designed in accordance with a single, coherent, intelligent plan and that this plan, to put it briefly, is man—or rather, the God-Man and those who are his.

Whereas we feel that we are simply may-flies in a huge world which is blind and deaf to man, Paul sees God, the Creator, and his first thought, and that is his Son who is to become a creature, a man, and the men who belong to him. And therefore the whole world was designed in view of this man, centred about him—designed too in view of man who God knew would use his freedom to become a sinner and a being in need of redemption. So that all God's creation was arranged from the first to suit this poor man, this sinful man. Hence Paul says that this creation was subjected to futility, but hopes to be set free from its bondage to decay and obtain the glorious liberty of the children of God.

Natural history—as we might say—and the history of mankind, natural history and the history of salvation and damnation, were ordered to each other from the first by the one God and Lord, who will not dismiss even sinful man from his service, who contrives to turn even the No of his free creature into the greater Yes of God and his mercy. That is why God was able to subject this earthly world to nothingness, bondage, and futility, because all this nothingness and futility, this mortality, this finitude, this death, is girt about by God's mightier power, which has instilled into this hopelessness the hope of a blessed freedom and a glory destined by God's grace for those who shall have been his children, brethren of the incarnate God, fellow-heirs of Jesus Christ.

So it is that with an eye and an ear which have been opened by God's revelation, Paul is able to gaze into all creation, listen to it, perceive its nothingness but also its yearning for the final glory which it is to share with the redeemed, transfigured sons of God. So he says: "We know that the whole creation has been groaning in travail together until now." Only it? No, we as well, although we are the sons of God. Within us too is this groaning and desire, because we have not yet reached the consummation. "And not only the creation, but we ourselves, who have the first fruits of the Spirit, groan inwardly as we wait for adoption as sons, the redemption of our bodies." Thus for Paul the heart of man, the heart of nature, and revelation are all agreed; the ultimate promise, ultimate light, unbounded hope are already rooted in our heart and in all nature. But everything is still at its beginnings, still in transition. Everything is still in the birthpangs of the new and perfect creation.

Is this what we feel our life to be like? Or does this "unitary" sense of existence which the Apostle has, and which binds together the blessedness to come and the anguish of the present in one elemental act of redeemed creation—does it disintegrate with us, so that at one moment we enjoy creation as though it were the ultimate things, and at another moment suffer on its account as though it bore no hope in its entrails?

All too easily that can happen to us. We either snatch

at the cup of the joys of this life as though nothing else existed for us to desire, or we curse the cup of sorrow, distress, and death as though it were not the only cure for those who must recover for eternal life.

Let us learn from St Paul, through this eighth chapter of Romans, where we really stand. We are redeemed souls who must make our way through an earthly world and see it for what it is: a world which is to share in the glory of the children of God and therefore even now is full of promise. But we must go further and have the courage to believe, be vigilant, and long for the glory of the children of God which is yet to be revealed in us. That is why—as St Paul says elsewhere—we are to rejoice; and even when we weep we must not weep as they do who have no hope. We must be composed, integrated people, because it is in us, the children of this earth who have the Spirit of the eternal God, that the world itself is integrated, knit together into a good world which is one day to find beatitude with God in his everlasting life.

THE CHANCE OF A LIFETIME

Rom 12:6–16

(Second Sunday after Epiphany)

The first eleven chapters of the letter to the Romans are of a doctrinal nature. From the twelfth chapter onwards, as is his custom, St Paul admonishes Christians about their moral obligations. Our text belongs to this second part of the letter. In itself it does not call for much explanation. It is intelligible and beautiful; it describes Christian life as it should be, in St Paul's view. We shall only add two brief observations.

In verses 6 to 8 Paul says, giving certain concrete examples, that we ought to have a bold confidence in our own mission and vocation. He has already said in verse 4: "For as in one body we have many members, and all the members do not have the same function, so we, though many, are one body in Christ, and individually members one of another." And then our text begins: "Having gifts that differ according to the grace given to us, let us use them." Then Paul says: "If prophecy, in proportion to our faith; if service, in our serving; he who teaches, in his teaching; he who does acts of mercy, with cheerfulness." Now when Paul says that everyone has his own gift, his own vocation, it is a truism. Every individual has his own quite particular character and experience, his own history, his own age, this or that sex, his own education and training, his own quite definite place in human society and—as Paul says—in the Church of God. But are we always well content with this place, this vocation and mission? The vocation and character that we have been given need not relate to the spiritual offices St Paul speaks of here. A person with the most secular and earthly of jobs to do is as much called by God as anyone; he is following his vocation. So these first three verses say to us: Do your job, accept it, do not look for anything else, do not dream of something you have not got and can never have. Do what you are called to by the reality of your life, perhaps even by the sheer force of your circumstances. Thus St Paul speaks to slaves in 1 Corinthians. Do that, he says. If you must admonish, then do it; if you have to speak, then do it. St Paul says this to us, who try to escape ourselves and our real lives. Whatever we have to do is a vocation from God. It is the chance of a lifetime; our one chance to be Christian.

What Paul says in verses 9 to 16—I mean his second observation—is also an appeal for bold confidence that ordinary, daily life is the stuff that makes up real Christianity. When he tells us here: "Rejoice with those who rejoice, weep with those who weep. Live in harmony with one another. Contribute to the needs of the saints. Be patient in tribulation. Rejoice in your hope. Serve the Lord," what else is this but a picture of our daily life, our daily life well-spent, to be sure, accepted with its joy and its tears, with the tribulation and distress of others, with the hospitality we extend, with the situations we would gladly escape, where we are expected to do plain little things and are tempted to dash out far beyond our depth. Is our love not often pretence? Do we honour one another? How zealous are we? Are we not often lukewarm? Do we

serve the Lord in all things? Or are we not often glad to
be able to shut the door behind us and leave others to shift
for themselves? Have we ever actually prayed for our
enemies, real or supposed? Do we rejoice with those that
rejoice, or do we expect others to rejoice in our own joy?
Do we weep with those who weep, or do we avoid becoming involved in other people's pain, saying to ourselves that
our own burden is quite enough for us to bear?

In these plain verses St Paul tells us: Love ordinary
things and ordinary life. Let life carry you along, with its
ups and downs, its people, its laughter and its tears—all
the variety that God's providence means it to have. Let
love be genuine, and then you will be Christians. If we
would only accept our gift and vocation, accept our
ordinary life as God's charisma, our burden would be
eased and we should be happy in this world.

GOD CHEERFULLY PUTS UP WITH US

Rom 12:16–21

(Third Sunday after Epiphany)

Verses 16 to 21 of chapter 12 form a kind of paragraph in the letter to the Romans which we could simply entitle: Loving our neighbour or loving our enemies.

At first glance this passage may seem to be nothing out of the ordinary. Good heavens, why not advise Christians to be peaceable so far as they can, even with bad neighbours? Why not recommend living a quiet life, stretching a point, giving in on occasion? After all, everybody knows it is the wiser man who gives in, though nobody wants to be the one to do it. If we interpret the text in this way, its lesson seems obvious enough. Not repaying evil for evil, being intent on good, refraining from strife, leaving vengeance to God, even doing good to an enemy on occasion—all fair enough. This last admonition might be thought to involve rather more than do the maxims of everyday prudence; yet Paul seems to base it too on perfectly sober practical considerations, when he says: "For by so doing you will keep burning coals upon your enemy's head"—you will make him feel ashamed, and, Paul obviously thinks, as often as not make him realize that you wish him well and that therefore there is no point in his continuing to be your enemy. "Overcome evil with good," says St Paul. Simple enough: good horse sense.

And yet, have we often tried it out? Can we say without more ado that we have overcome evil with good? In this world evil of whatever kind you will has an uncanny power; and part of its power is this, that when it attacks a man, even an innocent man, it involves him, the victim, in evil too. It really seems to be true that one must fight fire with fire, evil with evil, that to allow oneself to be put upon is to play the fool. Not that St Paul is an absolute pacifist, preaching unqualified non-resistance as a rule of life. This is not his attitude. In chapter 13, close upon these verses, he speaks of authority that bears a sword, that can use force, that must punish, that we must be subject to for conscience' sake, that can exact respect. Accordingly when Paul says here that we are to overcome evil with good, he does not mean that we must practise absolute non-violence at every juncture in practical life. But he does mean that a man proves himself a Christian by overcoming evil with his own goodness; by not answering a harsh word with harshness, one unloving word with another; by holding his peace when he has been grieved, not even complaining to another about what has happened; by patiently bearing with his neighbour, though the neighbour does not even realize he is a trial to anyone; that by this ampler, purer, selfless, silent goodness a man as it were causes evil to sink back into its own nothingness; he snuffs out evil, he turns it into good. Now this is a proper attribute of God. It is God who holds his peace and waits, is patient and forgiving; who draws good out of evil; whose goodness, forbearance and magnanimity let man follow evil, as it were, to the point of absurdity, where he realizes that he cannot go on that way any longer, turns about, and strikes out in a new direction. When we are going astray, God does not always choose to be stern, placing some insuperable obstacle in our path. Crushing evil is not the only way he has of dealing with it: he is a more gracious goodness, a holier justice, that can turn even evil into good. Though Paul also speaks of the day of wrath, he says in this passage: And so we ought to imitate the goodness of God, which does away with the evil of this world. That is no small task. I think we shall all have to admit that we have never done it yet. Many a time in our daily lives we have an opportunity to be patient with others, to be kind though they are not, to refrain from giving tit for tat, to be considerate and helpful to people who are unlikely to do the same for us. And perhaps those closest to us, even our best friends, are the people most difficult for us to put up with; perhaps we only manage it by holding our tongue. Well, if so, then we may hope that God will put up with us too. If we are so often a burden even to ourselves, must we not often be a fearful burden to God? (Humanly speaking, of course; but we *may* speak humanly of God.) He endures us patiently and cheerfully, rather like a loving mother who understands her child and his ways, even if he is obstinate, foolish and capricious. We can count on God's being patient with us in that way, count on it joyfully, even—we could almost say—with a holy shamelessness; for God is truly long-suffering and forbearing. But tell me, must not those near to us—and far from us—be able then to count on such a frame of mind in ourselves? We expect it of others as a matter of course; and if others treat us so, then they say nothing about the fact; it seems to us the most natural thing in the world and we take no notice. Now if we once start sternly demanding this attitude of ourselves, then it may dawn on us that many a good soul treats us with longanimity and forbearance, and never a word about it. Then we shall be more grateful, and find the burden that others lay on our shoulders a little lighter and less irksome, even find that is the yoke of Jesus Christ, a burden of grace which instructs us, enables us to keep our balance, makes us more mature and more humble, makes us love God more. If we act on it in the plainest, most ordinary way, the simple little lesson of today's Gospel will bring us very close to God's heart.

WHAT WE MUST GIVE AWAY

Rom 13:8–10

(Fourth Sunday after Epiphany)

The text set before us today says: "Owe no one anything, except to love one another; for he who loves his neighbour has fulfilled the law. The commandments, 'You shall not commit adultery, You shall not kill, You shall not steal, You shall not covet', and any other commandment, are summed up in this sentence, 'You shall love your neighbour as yourself.' Love does no wrong to a neighbour; therefore, love is the fulfilling of the law."

Reading over that text, we do not find it particularly hard to understand. It does not seem obscure. All the same, if we ask exactly what St Paul means when he says that love is the fulfilling, the fullness, the perfection of the law, we shall find that the matter is not so simple after all. And even if we reflect a while upon these three verses, we shall not really be able to say that we have got to the bottom of them. Perhaps we can understand these verses better if we glance at what went before. You remember that the third part of the letter to the Romans, chapter 12 to chapter 15, verse 14, deals with the moral duties of Christians. In the first seven verses of this thirteenth chapter St Paul has spoken of the duties of Christians towards civil authority, widening his horizon in the last verse to consider our

duties towards mankind in general. Thus he says in verse 7:
"Pay all of them their dues, taxes to whom taxes are due,
revenue to whom revenue is due", and now taking the
wider view, "respect to whom respect is due, honour to
whom honour is due." A very comprehensive precept, a
dictum recalling that of the old Latins, "to each his own".
Owe no one anything. Give everyone his due. If a man can
rightly claim a tax from you because he is an official of the
State, well and good. The State shall have its tax. If you
owe a man respect, show him respect. Now we might be
tempted to say: Once everyone has had his due from us,
there is an end to it. We owe nothing more, we have given
all that can be claimed from us. We may well think to
ourselves: Fine, now be on your way. All accounts are
settled. You have had all you can require of me, and I have
probably had all I can require of you. That is that. Oh
no, says St Paul, you have not started yet. When I have
treated the next man fairly, paid him my bills, refrained
from stealing his property, respected him, perhaps helped
him in one way or another as he can expect me to do, says
St Paul, then my obligations to him begin. Now what can I
still owe a man once I have given him everything he has
a right to? Obviously the remaining obligation must be of
quite a different sort. Paul says: "Owe no one anything."
Let us try translating the text somewhat differently, say
as follows: Pay every man his due in tangible terms, and
something will still be owing. What is that? Brotherly
love, says St Paul. Now if we examine our consciences and
allowed our real thoughts expression, we should probably
say: I am already practising this love. I have paid my
taxes, been respectful, given men due honour, done this or
that work of mercy, contributed to the support of my
pastors, given a shilling or two for the refugees, and so

forth. What more is expected of me? Paul says: Pay every man his due, and something will still be owing—agape, true love of our neighbour. Now how is that debt paid? In the case we are envisaging there is nothing more I can give; all that I have given is gone, the other man has tucked it all away—from bills and taxes to respect, honour, and even reverence. Supposing that I do still have to love him as my neighbour, as St Paul says, what more can he expect of me than I have already given him? Yourself. Only if we meditate on this can we understand Paul's saying that when all debts are paid and nothing is left outstanding, we still owe the other man fraternal love. It is true that we do. For this agape—a word which the Greeks do not seem to have used in this Pauline sense at all—, this love, has its origin, its being, and its prototype in God, of whom St John says that he is love, agape, and of whom St Paul says that his love, his agape, is poured forth in our hearts.

What is this divine love? It is God's surrender of himself to us. He not only gives us his gifts, he gives us himself. And if we are to love our neighbour with such agape, then our obligation is never satisfied. It keeps growing as we pay. We have never done with it. We can never say: Now be off, you have had all you can expect of me.

If I must give myself to the next man, can I say that I have done it? Obviously not. Why not? Well, to look at the matter from below, as it were, we are human beings, capable of this act of love towards men only in space and time, in earthly and tangible terms, wrapped in the payment of other debts. If only for this reason, our love remains something imperfect. When we look into our own hearts, how difficult the whole thing is; we cannot seem to get away from ourselves, we are always turning back to ourselves, we do not seem able to give our hearts away. And sometimes when we think that we have done it, is the truth not that we want the other man to give himself to us but have no mind to give ourselves to him just as he is?

Now looking at the matter from above, we see that we must be agrowing, always as it were absorbing infinities into ourselves because it is our business to remain open to God. For having given us himself in his agape, he belongs to us. And so our life, our being, is full of endless potentialities that we exploit only by degrees, step by step, piecemeal. If we keep enriching ourselves in this way, accumulating grace and blessing, ever more selfless and more faithful, absorbing God who gives himself to us, then we begin to see the kind of love we could give away to others, simply by giving away ourselves, still half-grown, still tentative, still imperfect though we are. At best, our achievements in this world remain so fragmentary, we are so pitifully imprisoned within ourselves. When we give to others it is usually from afar, to show them that we really do want to love our neighbour. And when we try to give from nearerby, try to show with words, or sacrifice, or faithfulness, that we want to love one another, it all remains so elementary. Now perhaps we understand a little better what St Paul means when he says: This love is the surpassing fulfilment of the law. Where laws are nothing more than laws, they can only represent a kind of rough-and-ready justice, distinguishing what is mine and what is the other fellow's, showing the individual what concrete goods and services he owes his neighbour. But exact calculations and legality are superseded when love enters the picture, when man gives himself with all his divine infinity to his neighbour, or at least tries to start doing so. Then he is no longer a man accomplishing something or rendering a service; he does more than comply with an objective norm which is equally binding on us all; he is a man perfecting himself by being the unique creature he is meant to be, perfecting himself because God has given him his own divine self in a unique way. And because what is involved here is a person, unique and irreplaceable, a person who achieves and perfects himself by lovingly giving himself away to others, all mere legality is superabundantly fulfilled and left behind. Thus love is the fulfilling of the law and the bond of perfection, as Paul says—that which will not pass away. That is why Paul can actually say: such a man has not only kept the law but more than fulfilled it, has passed beyond it and arrived at what must be a man's destination. For if we truly love our neighbour in God—only in God are we able to give ourselves away to our neighbour—, we really need not trouble about anything else. Law, with its demands, its over-harsh requirements, lies behind us. We have entered upon the blessed freedom of God's love for us, of our love for God, of the love that by God's grace we have for our neighbour. Only when we have got that length—not by our own powers but by the grace of God—shall we have reached our fulfilment in God.

WHAT IF THERE WERE
NOTHING MORE TO DO?

Rom 13:8–10

(Fourth Sunday after Epiphany)

Today's text is taken once again from St Paul's letter to
the Romans. It comprises only three verses of chapter 13.
Between chapter 12 and these verses Paul has spoken of
the duties of Christians towards authority, saying in that
connection—so we might well sum up his teaching—,
"Pay all of them their dues, taxes to whom taxes are due,
revenue to whom revenue is due, honour to whom honour
is due." Now he adds a few important admonitions about
the Christian love of our neighbour. We have often spoken
before of this love of our neighbour; but the Apostle and
the Church tell us the same thing again and so we shall
listen to these verses. They can always teach us something
useful. If the repetition should seem boring to us, we can
recollect what the beautiful tradition tells us about St John.
He used to keep saying "Little children, love one another";
and when his disciples asked why he always preached the
same thing, he replied that it was the commandment of
the Lord and that that was enough.

If we would meditate on the theology these three verses
contain, we might again try re-arranging them. In verse
10 St Paul says that love is the fulfilment of the law. Now
first of all that simply means that a man who loves his

neighbour and does what love bids him do has done what
the law requires of him; he has observed and fulfilled the
prescriptions of the law. And so love is the fulfilling of
the law. Looking at love from this point of view we might
think to ourselves: It is only a general term that comprehends the individual commandments and the various
duties we have towards God and, in particular, towards
our neighbour. We might suppose that this commandment
merely tells us to give him what is his due, as Paul says. If
we owe him attention, then attention; if we owe him taxes,
then taxes; and once we have discharged these individual
duties, so that we owe our neighbour nothing more, we
might suppose that we have fulfilled the other commandments and have done with them.

No doubt St Paul means by verse 10 that we must at
least do those deeds, acquit ourselves of those tasks of love,
and—why not say it—that it is always suspicious when
we appeal to our good heart and good intentions in order
to get out of doing the deeds of love. What we must do
is love in such a way that our love does fulfill the other
commandments. But Paul says something rather different
about love in verse 9. He says that it sums up the law. Here
he uses a Greek word that means providing something
with a head or a summing-up. Only in one other passage
of the New Testament does this word occur—in Ephesians
1:10. There Paul says that the Lord, Christ, unites the
universe in himself because it has pleased God to unite all
things, the universe, in the incarnate Word of the Father as
in their one head. Christ sums up the history of God's
redemption, God's mercy, the Church, and the whole of
creation: In him all things subsist and hold together, are
united, have their ultimate meaning and orientation, their
salvation and their end—in him, because he is at once

God and a creature. Now it is in this sense, says St Paul, that love is the head, the summing up, of the law. Only in love do the various individual prescriptions, rules, provisions, and demands find their ultimate meaning, are they united and transcended. For Christ is more than the sum of all other creatures. He is the super-eminent head. He is the summing-up which is more than the sum of all other things that are summed up. And so love is more than the sum of the commandments, more than the sum of all the things that we must do for our neighbour. It is all-embracing—because it is the love of God which he gives us and which we give him in the power of his Spirit. And so this love is really the very mystery of God, who is love. And because it draws God into its own being as its own source and goal, it is always something more than the rational order of the universe; more than the sum of tangible, calculable duties that we owe our neighbour; more, we might say, than the rules for keeping the machinery of this world and human life running smoothly. It is the unspeakable and the overwhelming, that which takes one into the depths of God himself. It is something that cannot be explained in terms of anything else. Though it does demand concrete deeds of loyalty and kindness to others, the core of it cannot be recast in any other mould. If we speak of God, or love, or the mystery of human life, or eternity, we are speaking of one and the same thing, in which everything is summed up as in its head. And so, as verse 9 says, love sums up the law.

Now we can also understand verse 8. There Paul says, pursuing the train of thought in the previous passage that I have already discussed, that we are to owe no one anything; as he has said, we are to pay taxes to whom taxes are due, honour to whom honour is due—in short, to pay our debts. And then do we owe no one anything further? If we examine our lives we are likely to discover that our attitude is that of the man in the Gospel: "Friend, what do I owe you? Take what belongs to you, and go." We have often said this, not only to our neighbour but even to God: Take what belongs to you; there you are, and (perhaps we do not add aloud) leave me in peace. This is often our attitude towards our neighbour and God and our life and our work—towards everything. There is a great deal that we are compelled to give; we have never done with paying taxes. So Paul says: Give this man what is due him, and the other man what is due the other man. And then he says: Owe no one anything. But no sooner has the Apostle said that than he stops short, and then goes on: "except to love one another." For we always owe this love. Such is Paul's mind, and that is why he says at this point that all things are summed up in Christ and in love. Not as though we did not have to give proofs of our love; but it is an unlimited and endless duty, done only when we loved God and our neighbour with our whole heart and our whole strength forever. Love is what we always owe. We can never really pay off that debt. Yet after all to realize the fact is not a grief, but a joy. Where should we be if once no more love were expected of us and we had done everything? We should be drained dry, finished, at the end of our rope. We should be dead men, nothing any more. But if there is such a thing as a love that never ends so long as God demands it of us, never ends because he always demands it of us, because he gives it to us so that we in turn can give it; if he promises through his very demand, that he will give us this boundless love for him and our neighbour; and if God's word is more reliable than our experience of our own niggardly, dying hearts;

if it is true that over our lives there hovers a boundless love which is never exhausted, which gathers everything into the infinite mystery of God—then we can believe and hope and love. Then what St Paul says is true: Love never ends. Then we can always owe God this love, and he will give us all eternity to go on loving him.

WE KNOW OURSELVES LEAST OF ALL

1 Cor 4:1–5

(Fourth Sunday of Advent)

In the fourth chapter of the first letter to the Corinthians St Paul writes: "This is how one should regard us, as servants of Christ and stewards of the mysteries of God. Moreover it is required of stewards that they be found trustworthy. But with me it is a very small thing that I should be judged by you or by any human court. I do not even judge myself, but I am not thereby acquitted. It is the Lord who judges me. Therefore do not pronounce judgement before the time, before the Lord comes, who will bring to light the things now hidden in darkness and will disclose the purposes of the heart. Then every man will receive his commendation from God."

About the year 55 A.D. at Ephesus, St Paul wrote his first letter to the church he had founded at Corinth on his second missionary journey. This letter deals with the practical concerns and difficulties of the new community, surrounded as it was by a pleasure-loving pagan metropolis. First Paul describes certain abuses which had crept in. Then he takes up questions of a more theological nature that had been put to him by the community. The first abuse, which Paul addresses himself to in the first four chapters of his letter, was a certain factious spirit within the community: some adhered to Paul; some to a preacher named Apollo who had arrived there later; some claimed to be special followers of Cephas—Peter; some again of Christ. Paul denounces this partisan attitude and says: "When all is said and done, we are all of us only servants of the Lord and stewards of God's mysteries. We have but one commission from one Lord; that commission we must faithfully carry out; and if we do so faithfully we need apologize to no man, we need take no heed of any human condemnation; our judge is the Lord. It is nothing to us if you judge us or differentiate between us, as though one of us were something more and the other something less, as though one were more important to the Christian body than the other. This text as such does not seem to be a particularly suitable one for Advent. Clearly it was chosen because of the one statement that the Lord will come and bring to light the things now hidden in darkness and disclose the hidden purposes of the heart, as the aged Simeon foretold in the Temple at the Lord's presentation. Paul of course has in mind the second coming of Christ. But since the Church rightly associates the first and second coming of Christ in her Advent liturgy, it is fitting to read this text in Advent.

Well then, our text tells us something that is of great importance. Paul writes that it is a small thing to him to be judged by any human court. His judge is the Lord, and it is the Lord he must please. Here, as it were to reinforce his point, he says that he does not even judge himself. Now such a statement needs to be interpreted with care, according to St Paul's own mind. In the same fourth chapter of First Corinthians which contains this strange statement, Paul stresses the fact that he is an apostle, that the Corinthians can learn something from him, and he explains in detail how he has become a spectacle to the world, even to angels, and to men. So he knows what he is and he is emphatic that his conscience is clear. He says that he has worthily carried out his apostolic office; and therefore he does judge himself after all. In one sense this is perfectly natural: Man is a free, spiritual being; he is responsible for his manner of life, and so inevitably he looks back at his past from time to time and considers whether he has been found a good and faithful servant. We ourselves do this, and we may say that even the Christmas season is a time of quiet, inward self-examination. Yet Paul says that he does not judge himself. What does he mean?

What he means may be of no small importance to us personally. He knows that the ultimate, irrevocable judgement, which exposes everything and judges everything, is not man's to pass but God's. God judges; at the end of the day it is he who knows our hearts and not we; he searches out all that is hidden, as Paul says, and brings it to light. That is something beyond us, even if we are meant to have a clear conscience and must often examine ourselves, as St Paul says elsewhere in this letter that a man should examine himself, for example, before approaching the sacrament of the Eucharist. Important as it is, however, this examination can take us only part of the way. There comes a point where we are the people least known to ourselves. There comes a point where we can no longer act as law and judge, prosecutor and accused, all wrapped up in one. And because this is so, our self-examination is something tentative and we may tranquilly leave God to be the judge. Sometimes we human beings are too anxious. We may be trying to get everything too tidy, to get the book-keeping of our interior life right to the last farthing. Of course there are people who do too little, who are superficial and too readily satisfied with themselves, who gloss over the dark side of their lives with a few facile excuses. But there are also the fretful, the anxious, the scrupulous, who somehow or other seem to think they must defend themselves against God. Whereas all we can do is flag to God and his mercy. Poor helpless frail creatures, we can only beg him to make the crooked straight, to bring low the mountains, to make the darkness light. If we look at what St Paul says from this point of view, then our text is a good one for this Christmastide. Let us really listen to the message of the Gospel, that God is kind, that he is coming to us in his incarnate mercy, and that when he comes he—not we—will bring what is dark into the light, bring what is hidden into God's day. This day, which judges us at this season if we truly celebrate Christmas, is the day of God's mercy, love, and faithfulness towards us. God stands by us even if we cannot always be said to have stood by him. He loves us, even if we are sometimes strangely forgetful of him in our daily lives, even if our heart seems to be more attached to many things than to him, the God of our heart and our portion forever. He is the one who is faithful to us, good to us, close to us, merciful to us. He is our light. He has come, and always longs to come to us more abundantly. We should be optimistic about God and his mercy; for we have no right to entertain a low view of God and his mercy. We do not judge ourselves. If instead we let him judge us, being patient with him and with ourselves, faithful to him, accepting the life that he himself accepted when he became man, trusting in him, then his judgement when his day comes will be grace and peace from God our Saviour.

WE NEVER KNOW WHEN LIGHTNING
WILL STRIKE US

1 Cor 9:24–27; 10:1–5

(Septuagesima)

Today's text is taken from St Paul's first letter to the Corinthians. Whereas other writings of St Paul are either very personal letters of his to a church or an individual, or else deal with one particular subject, the first letter to the Corinthians—and to some extent the second also—takes up a series of unrelated questions and difficulties that had happened to arise in this metropolitan Christian community.

In chapters 8 to 10 of this letter Paul discusses the question of food that has been offered to idols. May a Christian eat meat that has been sacrificed to the gods during an act of pagan worship? To this eminently practical question, which fairly bristles with difficulties, St Paul devotes three chapters, and today's text is drawn from those chapters. On the one hand Paul was magnanimous in this matter. He was not a timid soul. He was not the man to maintain that the narrowest, harshest, most inexorable principle must be the right one. In practical matters he allowed the utmost possible freedom; he did not imagine that heroism must be demanded of Christians at every turn. He was considerate and level-headed. Yet the Apostle knows that Christianity does call for heroism, not because

there is an ultimate point where a man must halt in God's
name, but because Christianity is a categorical decision for
God and his will. And Paul knows that there comes a time
when there is nothing for it but to decide whether one wants
to be a Christian or not. This is the context in which he is
speaking now.

Perhaps we could put the marrow of today's text in the
following way: Paul tells us something here about the
gravity of the absolute decision which has to be made
sooner or later in every human life. And because he understands that gravity, the Apostle—like the Church in every
age—is not surprised that the Christian keeps encountering
situations which seem vexatious, which he would fain
avoid, which involve this radical, inexorable decision—and
that over what seem to be trifles, or over obscure moral
questions that could apparently be debated forever, so
that if a man did not care to make his decision he could
keep finding new grounds for putting it off or taking the
easy way out. No, says Paul. And he gives us illustrations,
first from the sport that was popular in the great cities of
that age, and then from the Old Testament. No, says Paul.
There are moments of decision when all that is left to
one is either to remain inflexibly faithful to God and his
will, so that one simply cannot do a given thing, or to
attempt a compromise at the price of one's salvation. The
example which Paul cites from the world of sport does not
really seem to go to the heart of the matter. There is a race
in the stadium. Naturally there will be one winner, the one
who finishes first. The others also run; they will be second
and third and will receive honourable mention; after all
they are great athletes. Now our life is not quite like this.
The example is not particularly apt, for in human life
everybody is running his own race. A man is not compared

with others; he either arrives and is the victor or does not and loses everything. That is really the point Paul has in mind. In Christian life everybody can be a winner and be crowned with the laurel of eternal life. But one can also lose the day and be utterly defeated, not coming in second or third but forfeiting absolutely everything. And this is the lesson of our lame comparison. Everything in this life is so mixed up.

There are no utter geniuses and utter dolts. Nobody is so poor that he could not be poorer, nobody so rich that he would not like to be richer. Nobody loves God so much that he could not love him more. In this world there is nobody totally destitute of goodness, whose heart is no longer capable of any spark of longing for God. And so it is difficult for us to understand that our life centres more and more exclusively and radically upon one great question, even though we remain quite unaware of the fact, though we seem to go on and on in a world where there is no such thing as black and white, only various shades of grey. And yet all the while we are approaching a situation (even if it is met with in all its starkness, as it were, in purgatory) where we shall either have loved God with all our heart and all our strength or be lost. We need not be anxious. We too are wandering in the wilderness, as Paul reflects in the second part of today's text, for we are the people of God. And though God, the maker of things visible as well as things invisible, has built us a house on this earth that we love and feel is our home, we still remain pilgrims here, in search of our true country. On and on we go through the wilderness. Paul says: During their years in the wilderness—which were only a foreshadowing and parable of ours in the desert of this life—most of them were not pleasing to God. I say: We too are on a journey, on pilgrimage between time and eternity, earth and heaven; we have much to do; at God's word we must keep dividing our heart; not only may we keep compromising, we must— dividing our heart, our time, our mind, and our strength, so that we finally perceive that we have no lasting city here and are still in search of the truly perfect one which God, and he alone, can give us. And yet in the midst of our lives, of our freedom and our struggles, we have to take a radical, absolute decision. And we never know when lightning will strike us out of the blue. It may be when we least expect to be asked whether we have the absolute faith and trust to say yes; when we must turn our backs on many things in order to cleave to God and his word in Jesus Christ.

Let us keep praying: God, give us the inner strength and steadfastness to keep our hearts awake, ready to say yes without reserve when the time comes to say it, despite all our worldly wisdom, all our contrivances, all our compromises; so that by your grace our poor divided lives may receive that perfection which can be ours for eternity.

A THING THAT IS TRANSPARENT
MUST BE EMPTY

1 Cor 13 : 1–13

(Quinquagesima)

Our text today is taken from the thirteenth chapter of St Paul's first letter to the Corinthians. Chapters 12, 13 and 14 deal with supernatural gifts that had been bestowed on the Christians of Corinth: prophecies, the gift of tongues, and other charismata of the Holy Ghost which God's Spirit had given for the building up of that young church. But for all these gifts, certain disorders had arisen. So Paul writes lest the charismatic gifts themselves should lead to confusion. He speaks of right order and the limitations of these gifts; he explains how they should be properly used for the benefit of the community. But to show Christians who attached great importance to charismata that there is something more vital and basic in Christian life, Paul says in the midst of his discussion of special graces that he will show them a more perfect way. This "Canticle of love" has three parts. First the Apostle says that without this love everything else in human and Christian life—God's charismata, even faith, even martyrdom—is worthless; that without love we are nothing. Next Paul enumerates the characteristics of this love, which—though he does not explicitly say so—unites us with God and men alike. And finally he says that love is the supreme good because it is the ultimate and all-embracing thing and never ends.

In these few minutes it will not be possible to expound this song of songs. We should not do justice to St Paul's words. One must read them oneself, meditate on them and take them to heart. But for today we might just consider the relation between knowledge and love. At the very outset of this song of songs St Paul says: "If I understand all mysteries and all knowledge, but have not love, I am nothing." In the third section he says that our knowledge is imperfect, that we only know in part, and that this remains the case so long as we are here on pilgrimage, far from the Lord; we know as children do, in childish terms; we see in a mirror, dimly and in parables. In the second section Paul has said that love rejoices in the truth. So all through this song of songs St Paul is thinking of the connexion between knowledge and love. We, then, who profess to seek the truth, who write on our university buildings that the truth shall make us free—we are told that our knowledge is fragmentary and that love is what really matters. Indeed, if we examine our text with care, we shall see something which is generally overlooked or misinterpreted: Paul means that even in the consummation to come knowledge is perfected only when it is done away with, so to speak; when it abandons itself, so to speak, in love. True, Paul says that then we shall know face to face, not in a mirror, not in riddles and parables, not in shadows, but just as we are known. Yet if we weigh the faith as a whole, we shall realize that Paul does not mean that mystery will cease to be mysterious, that we shall comprehend God and as it were exhaust his infinity. We know by faith that even when we see face to face we shall gaze on the incomprehensible God. To that extent, Paul means, faith and hope remain; for if we translate rightly—he does not say that faith, hope, and love remain "now" as contrasted with "later", the consummation; he says: "But now"— this is the particle which introduces a proof—"but now faith, hope, love abide, always abide." Of course this faith becomes a faith that sees face to face, and this hope becomes possession; but because this vision is the vision of the incomprehensible God and because this possession is the possession of the infinite God who must ever give himself anew in his sovereign love, there always remains something that can be called faith and hope—at least in the sense which Paul means here. Now the Apostle says that love is greater than faith and hope as they remain even in eternity, even in the vision of God face to face; even where mystery is close at hand, where it is looked upon, man's happiness can only consist in that vision—he cannot cease gazing into endless, unutterable mystery. Love rejoices in the truth because that truth is the disclosure of love's ineffable incomprehensibility even when one sees it face to face. Only where truth is transmuted into love, only where love can rejoice over truth because truth as it were hands over to love, only where knowledge is the affirmation of incomprehensible mystery—only there are consummation and beatitude, God and man with the mysterious secret they share: love. That is why Paul says: "So faith, hope, and love abide, these three: but the greatest of these is love." Then he adds one thing more: "Make love your aim", seek the mystery that lies beyond all dull knowledge, seek the mystery that nobody can understand because a mystery understood is one no longer and a thing that is transparent must be empty and futile. Make love your aim because that is the only perfection. Of course one may ask: What is love anyhow? And the answer must be: Everything, the all-embracing, that which comprehends all things and is not comprehended, God who is love, man who has attained to God in love, the unutterable. If we did not already know from experience what it means, no one could explain to us this saying: "Make love your aim." It would be Greek to us. But since God has already poured forth the Holy Spirit of his love into our hearts, these words mean something to the man who is sick with longing, who grieves over darkness, who rejoices in the truth, who struggles towards mystery and light inaccessible, so that it may one day be accessible and he may look upon it. If he reads the song of songs in faith and love, a stronger desire for the love that abides and is best of all will awaken in his heart. Make love your aim.

GOD'S TRUTH IN SEARCH
OF THE MOMENT

2 Cor 6:1–10

(First Sunday in Lent)

Let us consider together the first three verses in the sixth chapter of the second letter to the Corinthians. Only these. Paul says: "Working together with him, then, we entreat you not to accept the grace of God in vain. For he says, 'At the acceptable time I have listened to you, and helped you on the day of salvation.' Behold, now is the acceptable time; behold, now is the day of salvation." These are the opening verses of today's text. In the second letter to the Corinthians St Paul defends himself against adversaries that he has discovered in the church of Corinth. In his first seven chapters he celebrates the dignity and holiness of his apostolic office, and without any thought of self-praise candidly emphasizes the becoming attitude which he has shown in the sight of God and men in discharging his duties. Chapters 8 and 9 are a digression; here Paul discusses the collection that is to be taken up at Corinth for the church in Jerusalem. And in chapters 10 to 13 St Paul again joins issue with his opponents at Corinth. Describing the dignity of the apostolic office in these first chapters, he exalts it as a ministry of reconciliation and says that he not only preaches Christ but beseeches them on behalf of Christ to be reconciled to God betimes. So Paul does not merely preach some general reconciliation with God; he knows that he is proclaiming God's word in a very particular situation, at the right time on the day of salvation. His office has an extraordinary weight and urgency because the word cannot be preached anytime and anywhere, because it is not a truth for all times and therefore for none, but a truth that has come from God in search of a particular moment—the Christian moment—and therefore has found and ushered in that moment. Quoting Isaiah, chapter 49, in the Greek translation, St Paul uses a very precise Greek word that does not simply mean "time". He says "kairos". The word was familiar to the Greeks of that period. There was even a god called Kairos, whose statue stood at the entrance of the stadium at Olympus—the god of the right moment, of the ephemeral situation where time must be seized by the forelock, as we say. Naturally, Paul does not believe that such a god exists. But he does recognize the existence of this crucial, fleeting moment that God gives us, the moment of decision in human life. We all know that we only live once, and that this one life produces the fruit of eternity. We Christians know that this irrecoverable time is God's gift. We are called into a particular age and given a time there whose length God alone determines. We have no say in that. Every moment of this time is precious and unique, for no moment is ever really repeated. And since we Christians are called as Christians into the age of Christ, when God's revealed word about his redemption, his love and mercy is preached to us, and since God's incarnate Word belongs to this our age, the day of salvation is really here; this is the right moment, the acceptable moment, the "psychological moment" (as Paul's word might be rendered). So Paul says and the Church says, here on the threshold of Lent: Now is the right time, now is your kairos, now is the day of salvation. This now will not last for ever, this now is transitory, this now is a gift beyond our control. We may still have a long life before us, we may see many Lents to come; but all the same every moment of our life is precious, and everyone is a gift of God. We often wish we were living at some other period of history or of our own lives. Perhaps we are going through a time of distress and long for a time of joy. Perhaps we should be glad of a time for greatness and instead are tied down to some paltry, weary, monotonous job that seems to have very little point. Yet scripture says of every one of our moments: Behold, now is the acceptable time, now is the day of salvation—the day that you have now, the hour that is given to you now. We should keep begging God with all our strength: Give me the light and strength to see the time I have as you do, to recognize it—though it may be distressing or wearisome or bitter, may even be the hour to die or to endure a lingering death—as your hour and your gift, as the day of your salvation.

If we could begin every day in this spirit, could accept each hour from the hand of God (for that is where it comes from), if we did not complain, if we did not beat our heads against a stone wall, but said with faith and humility, in the power of the Spirit and the light of the Lord: Now is the day of the Lord, the hour of salvation, the moment that can produce my eternity—then should we not understand our lives better? Then would not our days, however empty of human consolation, be fuller, brighter, nobler, ampler, blessed with the secret blessedness that the Christian can know even in desolation, even on the cross? Let us say once more with the Apostle: Behold, now is the right moment; behold, now is the day of salvation. O God, by

your grace give us light and strength to recognize and
endure the day and the moment that you keep giving us
as your gift, your grace, and our appointed task, so that
this time, the time of salvation, may produce your eternity.

THE PAST IS THE KEY TO THE FUTURE

Gal 4: 22–31

(Fourth Sunday in Lent)

St Paul wrote the letter to the Galatians round about the year 55 B.C. while he was at Ephesus. We are not quite sure which churches in Asia Minor it was addressed to. In any case Paul had visited these churches twice, and after his departure certain Jewish Christian preachers arrived and taught these Gentiles that they could not really be complete Christians unless they accepted circumcision and other prescriptions of the Jewish law. Now Paul declares in chapter 1 of this letter that his gospel—the gospel of freedom from the law of the Old Testament—comes from God. In chapter 2 he says that his gospel agrees with the gospel of the original apostles at Jerusalem. And then he shows that according to God's Old Testament law itself, outwardly observing the law, observing the law without grace, does not justify a man; that only faith in the Holy Ghost, only the grace of Jesus Christ, justifies a man. Our text is part of St Paul's effort to prove by the Old Testament that Christians are freed from the yoke of the Old Testament.

If we read these verses we must admit that it is difficult for us to see Paul's meaning. He uses a type of theological proof which was a commonplace among the Jewish theo-

logians of that day. He draws a parallel; he cites an antetype
in the Old Testament which clarifies and illustrates something in the present dispensation, the New Testament. We
might say that he sets up two sides in the Old Testament:
on one side he has Hagar and her son Ishmael, on the other
Sarah and her son Isaac. These are types of the two Testaments or Covenants: the Old Covenant, the law which was
given on Sinai, and the New Covenant, the new law of
freedom and the Spirit—corresponding to the earthly
Jerusalem and the heavenly. Paul concludes that those who
belong to the Old Covenant are in bondage to the law,
whereas we who belong to the heavenly Jerusalem and the
law of freedom and the Spirit, are free in Christ. Now this
kind of reasoning may seem strange and artificial to us.
But the basic idea ought to be quite comprehensible. It is
an ancient one. When God acts, when he has acted, throughout the course of a long history, then we naturally expect
this whole action of his to have a particular style, a continuity and coherence. God, who has thought out this
single history, brought it into being, shaped and guided
it, governs all its thousand details and vicissitudes so that
everything fits into place. The future will always be new
and startling; we shall not be able to foretell it by studying
the past. But once it is here we see that, new as it may be,
it is still of a piece with the past; there is a normality about
it, an inner bond, that makes it part of the totality of that
history we are speaking of. We are justified, accordingly,
in discovering prototypes and likenesses of the present in
what has gone before. At the same time this history is ever
maturing, ever disclosing more of what it means, leaving
the past behind as a halting analogy, a feeble foreshadowing
of the fulfilment we know. Our present is Christ Jesus.
Within the unity of God's historical action, within the one

vast work of the God who gives all grace, what has gone before takes on a significance that is surprising and yet consistent with the rest. So in this strange doing of God there was one man who was the son of promise and another, the son of the bondwoman, who simply fell heir to his mother's lot. Here Paul can see a parable of the way God in the New Covenant calls men into the freedom of the Spirit, pardons them, delivers them from the yoke of a law imposed from without, giving them the inward Spirit of power, grace, and love whereby a man is able to satisfy the law superabundantly and interiorly, so that he is no longer the slave of the law but a son, doing what God's law in the Old Testament really intended, because of the intimate understanding, the empathy, he has with the Giver of the law.

Can we not discern such a continuity in God's gracious governance of ourselves and our lives? We too are always being startled, always having to enter situations we had not foreseen or reckoned with, we too must keep saying: I am never prepared for the way things turn out. But if they turn out as God, who is greater than we are and more mysterious, planned for us, and if we have accepted them and not frustrated God's design by indocility of heart, then we shall suddenly sense that it all fits into the mysterious pattern of our lives. Of course our life is still incomplete, a kind of jig-saw puzzle. If we study its composition we cannot really see how the pieces fit together or what the finished picture will look like. But if we look at our life with candour, humility, and love, we shall not fail to discern the unity of God's work in us. What once seemed glaring contradictions have already been reconciled. Much that once seemed hopelessly dissonant has already settled into harmony, thanks to God's goodness and mercy. This higher harmony may have been unexpected, it may be still incomplete, but at least enough of it is there for us to be able to feel confident of the rest. And much in the past can serve as a type and allegory of what now is and what is yet to come. Paul once said to his Christians: "I am sure that he who began a good work in you will bring it to completion." That is the motto of God's harmonious work within us. Because we know from experience that he is kind and forgiving, the God of enlightenment, mercy and all consolation, we can rightly read the present and the future in the light of the past. We too find types in the past of what is and what is to be. And when everything is over, it will all have fitted into the one, great, holy loving idea God had when he fashioned our being and our life, when he called us by name.

HE IS THE ONE WHO STARTED IT

Phil 1:6–11

(Twenty-second Sunday after Pentecost)

Our text comprises the introduction to this letter, apart from the address and the salutation. The church at Philippi had sent a representative to visit Paul in prison and bring him a contribution for his own support and for his work. Paul refers to this matter of his support, about which he will have more to say later. We shall glance at these verses and those immediately preceding, which are omitted in today's lesson, so as to round off our passage.

Paul is thinking of his community. It is his favourite, a flourishing community in the midst of its pagan environment, clinging to the word of faith and the Gospel hope, looking forward in love to the day they all await, whether it come in death or in the end of the world's history: the day of Christ. When the Apostle thinks of this community he can say: "I thank my God in all my remembrance of you." This gratitude for the vigour of the Gospel, for the good estate of the church, for the faith and love of the Philippians, quite naturally becomes a prayer; for Christians have not yet reached the end of the road, they must still fight and grow and increase so that they may be really perfected on Christ's day. So he continues: "Always in every prayer of mine for you all making my prayer with

joy." Can we say the same of our own prayer? Then he tells
the reason why he so joyfully gives thanks and prays for
this church. It is not simply their Christian life, their faith,
their conversion, but also the way they have associated
themselves with St Paul's missionary intentions, the way
they not only receive from him but also give, the way
these new converts feel they have a responsibility and a
mission, along with the Apostle, to this pagan world. That
is why they have prayed for him and supported him as well
with their material gifts. So Paul goes on: "Thankful for
your partnership in the Gospel from the first day until
now." He puts it very discreetly, almost in veiled language,
in very general terms; but he is not talking about some
abstract interest, he is talking about partnership in prayer
and about material support. Here is the reason for the
Apostle's gratitude and joyful prayer. What Paul sees in
this small alms—pleasing but in itself insignificant—is a
token, a tangible proof, an embodiment of their whole
attitude. And so his mind's eye is led from this little
offering to their whole Christian life, still agrowing, still
en route, still to be perfected, and he says: I am sure that
he who began the good work will bring it to completion
at the day of Jesus Christ.

We are all the work that God the Father has begun in
his grace through Christ Jesus in the Holy Ghost. *He* has
begun the good work in us, we have not. But he has begun
it through our freedom, and it is always questionable, as
it were—it is always the one great all-embracing question,
comprehending time and eternity—whether the work that
has been begun will be brought to completion. And when
the Apostle asks this question, when he asks whether what
he has begun with words and tears, with penance, anguish,
and all the power of his apostolic work and suffering, will

really be brought to completion or whether it will run down and atrophy—when he asks whether these men who have now made a start will one day enter the glory of divine light as children of the light, asks with fear and trembling because no man is certain of his salvation—then he lifts up his eyes to God, his heart is filled with confidence, and he says: I am sure that God, who has begun this work, will bring it to completion. And we too may say this, frail and helpless as we are, we whose Christianity is always running down and atrophying, we whom the stream of daily life is always threatening to swallow up, extinguishing whatever light and power, life and glory, has begun to emerge in our Christianity. Instead of studying ourselves we ought to say: He who has begun this work— and it is not we who have begun it, not we in our weakness, even in our freedom—God, in the glorious power of his grace, will bring it to completion. And that is our bold assurance, our splendid sovereign confidence. He says: It is right for me to feel thus about you all, because, he says—and here something entirely personal and genuinely human comes into the power and grandeur of God's work—because I hold you in my heart, for you are all partakers with me of grace, both in my imprisonment and in the defence and confirmation of the Gospel. Ah, if every priest could say that to his congregation! If God would grant the clergy everywhere the grace of such a relationship, both divine and human, with their people, so that each could say: You are all partakers with me in my work, in the defence and confirmation of the Gospel. And then he tells them again how he loves them and how close to them he feels: God is my witness. What Paul says here is not a pious cliché, not just the conventional language of the priest, preacher, and apostle. No: God is my witness, how

I yearn for you all—and we may quite legitimately translate the rest so: with the deepest love of Jesus's heart. Then he returns to what he has said at the beginning, that he prays for them with gratitude and joy.

And this is what he prays for: And it is my prayer that your love may abound more and more, with knowledge and all discernment. How strange, yet how splendid and how profound! I think it was Leonardo da Vinci who once said that love is the mother of all important knowledge, love and nothing else. May your love abound more and more with knowledge and all discernment. Only where love grows does true gnosis, true knowledge, grow; and God's grace gives one light to understand what man is before God only in proportion as one loves from the heart. And then Paul says that this knowledge that comes from love is given them, so that they may choose what is right. How difficult it often is for us to know what to do. Only the knowledge which is born of great love will really show us. And what will it all lead to, once love abounds more and more and the fair light, the joyous blessed light to see our life as God does, abounds in us and we keep choosing the right way at all the cross-roads of our existence? That you may be pure and blameless for the day of Christ, when he appears at your death or at his second coming, filled with the fruits of righteousness which come not from ourselves but through Jesus Christ, to the glory and praise of God.

We need add nothing more. This short passage, this little introduction to an affectionate letter of St Paul's to his favourite community, says enough.

WE SHOULD NOT FEAR HIS CLOSENESS

Phil 4:4–7

(Third Sunday in Advent)

The church at Philippi was the first Christian community in Europe. It was founded by St Paul on his second missionary journey, during a brief sojourn which had to be suddenly broken off. This flourishing community, where a truly Christian life was led, was St Paul's favourite church. Of course its members were human as well; there were small irritations and difficulties; but all things considered, it could fairly be described, in St Paul's phrase, as the crown of his apostolate. He writes to them from captivity, as his letter says, out of gratitude for the offering which a representative of the community has brought him. We do not know for certain where Paul was imprisoned. Perhaps this was the first captivity at Rome, but it may well have been an earlier one at Ephesus about which little is known. So Paul may be writing from Ephesus to his church in Europe. At all events it is a personal letter, an intimate letter. In it Paul does not deal with weighty matters of abstract theology, but heart speaks to heart. So the various parts of the letter are loosely connected. In one place Paul says something about himself, how he is, what he is doing, what his hopes are; he interpolates prayers; then he speaks of his expectations for the community, his gratitude to it; then he mentions various individuals among the Philippian Christians.

Thus today's text from Philippians is a short passage which is complete in itself. Let us just glance at it together. Paul says: "Rejoice in the Lord always." Yet another exhortation to us Christians to rejoice, to rejoice in the Lord, in the consciousness that we are united with Christ, live in him, act through his grace, and so rejoice through his grace. We are reminded to rejoice, admonished to rejoice; so to rejoice is a Christian virtue. There is no need to be reminded of, and admonished about, things over which we have no control. So if we must be reminded and admonished to rejoice, it is probably because we do not rejoice as we can and ought to do. Today, then, let us hearken to the Apostle as he urges us once more to rejoice in the Lord always. You see, he knows that this is easier said than done but at the same time it is important, and so he adds: "Again I will say, Rejoice." And now quite a different admonition follows: "Let all men know your forbearance," he says. Not everything the Christian cherishes, thinks, believes, practises, suffers, and hopes for is known to others and intelligible to them. For as Paul says in another passage: "The gifts of the Spirit of God are spiritually discerned. The spiritual man judges all things, but is himself judged by no one." But, Paul says here, others should always observe your goodness, your kindness, your inner peace and equanimity. They may not realize that these are especially Christian qualities, but that is neither here nor there. They must notice that you are considerate, helpful, benign, tranquil, self-possessed, candid, and loving. That is something anyone can see. The ultimate roots of it may not be apparent, but at least the prints of your Christianity must be seen. "Let all men know your forbearance", says St Paul. And who knows, they may have an inkling that our life is drawn from a deeper source than theirs. "Let your kindliness be manifest to all men", says Paul.

Strange, in the midst of these admonitions Paul interjects something that is not an admonition at all: "The Lord is at hand." How strange: when he is preaching about morals he thinks of Christ, when he is thinking about the Christians and when he is thinking about all the rest of mankind, he thinks of the Lord. He thinks of the Lord as of someone nearby, someone who once lived among us and has simply gone away and is in heaven; he thinks of the Lord as of one abiding with us in his Spirit, in his word, in his brother and in his sister, as of one who is coming, who would penetrate ever further into our lives, who would absorb our lives ever more completely in himself, who with his Spirit and his power, with his own history which is still going on, is engaged in one tremendous advent. And he is close to us as well, in the destiny that leads our lives towards a single goal, to death and judgement, which may be nearer than we think. The Lord is near. He is close to all of us. Are we close to him?

We ought not to fear this closeness. We should feel that it is a blessed, protective closeness, the closeness of our salvation, of our strength, the closeness of promise and fulfilment, the closeness of authentic reality, the closeness of all that draws to itself the whole fabric of our history and the narrow of our being; the closeness of our whole destiny. If we felt the closeness of the Lord in this way and if we were close to him in this way by faith, hope and love, then his closeness would be joy and peace to us. That is why Paul continues: "Have no anxiety about anything." He means that torturing, consuming, destroying anxiety that degrades a man and breaks him, that does not let him rise above his fate. He means the anxiety that pagans experience. This, he says, we are to have no part of. We should repudiate it. Are we light-hearted and untroubled people? Can we cheerfully face the day? Paul does not think so. He knows we have our worries; he knows that the pressure, the narrowness, the distress of life tell on us. All the same he thinks and says: "But in everything"—everything that worries, harasses, cramps, distresses or pains us—"let your requests be made known to God—with thanksgiving." All prayer should tell God our distress and so be candid and open, unconstrained and tranquil, calm and unanxious. In all prayer and supplication—with thanksgiving. Astonishing. When Paul is speaking of prayer, supplication, prayer that arises from the troubles of life, he thinks of thanksgiving, of "eucharist"—the word used here. When we pray, are we only little beggars before God, wrapped up in our own worries? Is our heart ever enlarged in thanksgiving, as it were a great preface in the eucharist of which our life is the celebration—thanksgiving that we Christians are created, called, sanctified, redeemed, pardoned, preserved, rescued in God's providence, that we are God's beloved children, that God's Spirit is given to us that eternal life awaits us, that the Lord is nigh, that he is kind and clement and that his mercy is unbounded? Do we ever give thanks that our thanksgiving and our petitions reach the ears of God, and that we ask God to perfect the good work which he has begun in us—and for which we are just thanking him—on the day of Christ that is not far off? "And the peace of God, which passes all understanding, will keep your hearts and your minds in Christ Jesus." So this peace is in Christ Jesus, to whom we belong, whom we love, whose body we receive. Ultimate, all-embracing peace we have in him. It surpasses all our thought, even all our desire. And accordingly we often hardly realize that we already possess it. Yet it is there, and Paul says of it: Let this blessed tranquillity which is God's peace stand guard, as it were, before your hearts to defend them, almost—the Greek word can bear such a sense—place our hearts under arrest and keep them in custody. The peace of God, after all, is not of our doing or making; it is God's doing within us, the doing of the power of his grace. And so we wish, pray, and supplicate that this mighty peace may as it were attack all our hearts in all its native force, guard the gate of the city of each heart, keep watch there lest any discontent, any animosity, any discord, any schism should creep in, any murmur of distrust of God, of our own life, or of our fellow-men, whereby we might lose this perfect peace. May the peace of God, which passes all understanding, keep your hearts—for if it keeps your hearts, then it will keep your minds, your projects, your decisions, and your desires—in Christ Jesus.

There is today's epistle. Let us turn it into a prayer so that our prayer and supplication may reach the ears of God, so that peace and joy in Christ Jesus may dwell evermore in our hearts, so that we may bless the eternal Father for calling us into the kingdom of the Son of his love, so that we may be at one and enjoy peace, and so that our Christian attitude in Christ Jesus may be plain to all other men through our forbearance and benignity, so that they too—whether or not they explicitly discover the Lord and his grace—may to some extent meet Christ in us, at least in that consideration and kindness which, human though they seem, are ultimately a fruit of God's grace. May that grace keep our hearts now and evermore.

THE NEW STYLE IN REMORSELESSNESS

Col 3:12–17

(Fifth Sunday after Epiphany)

During his captivity at Rome St Paul receives news from a Christian community in Asia Minor which he did not found himself. It was founded by a disciple. Paul's reply is this letter to the Colossians. In the first part of the letter he goes into certain misinterpretations, partly of Jewish and partly of gnostic origin, which were a danger to the community. He represents to them the surpassing dignity of Christ, which is not to be compared with any angelic principalities or powers that there may be in the world. These Colossians were tempted to reverence such angels and so to imagine that Christ was only one among the cosmic powers. In the second section, from chapter 3 onwards, Paul then discusses the moral life of the Christian, as he is fond of doing after the dogmatic part of a letter.

In chapter 3, verses 1 to 18, Paul considers the conduct of the individual; then towards the end of the chapters he considers the duties involved in the various states of life. Today's text occurs in the first part of chapter 3. It is full of beauty and meaning. It speaks to us as God's chosen ones, holy and beloved, and calls upon us to practise many virtues: compassion, kindness, lowliness, meekness, patience, love; to pursue peace, to pray, to sing spiritual songs—in a word, whatever we do in word or deed, to do everything in the name of the Lord Jesus.

Now we may be struck by something in the list of virtues which the Apostle commends to his community: he admonishes them to practise lowliness and then forgiveness: "Forbearing one another and, if one has a complaint against another, forgiving each other; as the Lord has forgiven you, so you also must forgive." So it is clear that when he inculcates peace it is not simply the peace of the individual heart within itself that is meant but peace among Christians. Does not Paul justify this admonition to peace by saying: "You were called in the one body?" Now it is extraordinary that in so short a letter, where there is so much to be said, Paul should urge mutual forbearance and forgiveness upon his readers. Let us picture this community for a moment: they are zealous souls; they are all Christians, recent converts full of the enthusiasm of the recent convert, who knows that he must shine like a star amid the darkness of the world; a community whose every member has become a Christian out of sheer conviction, in defiance of his whole environment. So this church takes its Christianity in deadly earnest; every member who has found his way to it knows that he shares with every other member the profoundest experience of his life—the tremendous decision for Christ and Christ's redemption. And yet Paul admonishes them to bear with one another and forgive one another. Not only that; he has the admonition on the tip of his tongue, as it were. It is not an admonition given in view of the peculiar circumstances of this one church; for he says practically the same thing in the letter to the Ephesians, chapter 4, verses 31 and 32. So it must obviously be an admonition appropriate and important to every Christian. If we turn to the sermon on the mount, we find

Jesus himself admonishing us to forgive one another and be reconciled. We find a kind of sequel to the doctrine of Jesus Sirach, chapter 28, in the Old Testament, which reminds and admonishes us that we can only beg God's forgiveness if we in our turn are prepared to forgive our fellow-men. The Lord even includes this petition, and this assurance to God that we forgive others, in Our Father. He tells us the parable of the unmerciful servant (Mt 18) to warn us that if we are unforgiving, God too will be so. In Matthew 18 the Lord tells Peter that we must forgive each other seventy times seven, which in plain English means till the cows come home. And in Luke he says: "Forgive, and you will be forgiven." Small wonder, then, if St Paul takes up Jesus's admonition to write it on the hearts of the Colossians. Is it an admonition that we too are ever and again in need of and must take to heart?

When all is said and done, we are the same sort of people as the people of that age, whom Jesus and Paul admonished. But if we are really to grasp what it means to be forgiving in our own day-to-day lives, it is important to realize that nowadays we have a different way of being irreconcilable: the style has changed. Where people live cribbed, cabined, and confined—on top of each other, as we say—or where people are very spontaneously vital and down to earth— and there is probably less of either thing today than there used to be—anger, hatred, rancour are very straightforward, concrete, and active. There you have the vendetta; implacable enmity is handed down from generation to generation; clan or tribal warfare is endemic; a man stands behind his father, his mother and his brother, and an enemy of his kin is his own enemy; there you have whole-hearted enmity to the death, or whole-hearted friendship and fidelity to the death. Among ourselves these things are no longer "done"; they are replaced, or at least discreetly veiled, by pale convention. We do not fall upon each other knife in hand; we do not take special precautions to ensure our status as guests so that we cannot be attacked; it is easier to withdraw from people and live aloof; we can more readily avoid each other. And so, I suppose, we hardly notice that this evangelic admonition speaks to our condition and that we by no means automatically comply with it. We may well say: What enemies, pray, have I? Whom do I refuse to forgive? It may be true that there are some things one cannot be expected to put up with. It may be a duty for me to stand up for my rights. It may simply be impossible to live in perfect peace with my neighbour. Even saints have sometimes gone to law in defence of their rights; sometimes they had no choice. And to draw the line at certain impositions may be an act of virtue that contributes to the Christian education of another. But precisely because there are such cases and because there is now a different way of being unforgiving and remorseless— a different style—, we may overlook the fact that we do not automatically comply with this admonition. For when today's text tells us that we are to forgive others as God has forgiven us, then obviously it places us in a delicate position. How has God forgiven us? Not by saying, as men do: We had better forget all about it. Not by saying, as it were: Oh, never mind. He does not forget that way. He forgives us by seeking us out, by loving us, by loving us with all his heart, by giving us everything—that is, himself. He forgives us by making something else out of our evil deed, our sin, the ill-will of our hearts, the injury we have done him, giving us another chance, a new start in life, for-giving without reserve and with all his heart, thinking of nothing now but mercy, compassion, love, and faithfulness unto the end, so that all that is left of the past is the goodness of it.

Do we forgive this way? Candidly and lovingly? Or do we avoid people if they are uncongenial, if they get on our nerves, if they have hurt our feelings at some time or other? Do we tolerate them on these terms, rather pleased with ourselves for not assaulting them or even saying anything injurious? And what of the state of our hearts? What judgements do we pass there? What of those secret thoughts? What is our real attitude towards people, there within our hearts? Do we accuse no one there? Do we really try to understand others? Have we ever tried to stand coolly aside from our anger, resentment, and pride and really study others; tried to understand them in the light of their ideas, their cast of mind, their dispositions, the kind of life they have led, their temperament, their upbringing and education, their experiences? Or do we think that our instructive reactions, as they say, are the best guide to judgement where people are concerned?

It is difficult to forgive and really bear with others. Let us not say "tolerate," which implies that the other person is a burden that really ought not to be thrust upon us. If we translate properly: "Bear with one another as Christ bears with you", as a patient, loving mother does with her child, then we shall perceive how difficult a thing is required of us. And yet to forgive in this way, not merely forgive the injuries done us but give ourselves to others and bear with them as God gives himself to us and bears with us, is the only way to comply with the admonition of the Gospel. It is hard. Only by God's grace can we be so selfless, only when God himself is our partner and God's freedom has become our own.

FORGIVING EACH OTHER

Col 3:12–17

(First Sunday after Epiphany)

Our text is taken from St Paul's letter to the Colossians. He writes from prison to a church in Asia Minor with which he is not personally acquainted, to warn them against entangling themselves in a misguided angel-worship, part Jewish and part gnostic, which seemed to threaten their faith in Christ the sovereign Lord and his redemption. Paul says: "Put on then, as God's chosen ones, holy and beloved, compassion, kindness, lowliness, meekness, and patience." We are God's chosen ones because he knows us, he has called us, he has conceived and planned our life, he leads us, he has given us a special vocation and even the grace to respond to it. And so we are holy, for we are consecrated and anointed by the Holy Spirit of God which is poured forth in our hearts. That is why we are truly God's beloved, loved with the unutterable love of God, the holy, the almighty, the everlasting. That is why Paul says that we must "put on" the inmost spirit of the virtues he enumerates. It is a startling image the Apostle uses here: "putting on". Exegetes have long been puzzled by this image. Elsewhere too St Paul speaks of putting on Christ. Possibly he had in mind some cultic gesture familiar to the pagan religions round about, whereby a person donned

the robes and symbols of a god and mimed him so as to
feel that he was in some sort transformed into the object
of his worship. However that may be, we have indeed put
on the Lord. We have been transmuted by his Spirit into
his image and likeness. We must live him, re-create his
image in us. Not, of course, by mere outward imitation,
an outward mime. We put him on in such a way that we
are actually drawn into him, we reflect his being and his
life and so prolong his life within history until he comes
again. And so we are to imitate his virtues. The virtues
St Paul enumerates here are social virtues, the virtues of
life lived in community as human beings and as Christians.
"Put on the inmost spirit of compassion, kindness, lowliness, meekness, and patience." We need not enlarge upon
these individual virtues. We all know how necessary they
are in our life with one another. We all know how difficult
they often are to practise, and so we can only acquire these
virtues—this patience, this kindness, this humble defer-
ence, this forbearance, this longanimity, this generosity of
heart as it were—if we put on Christ the Lord. "Forbearing
one another and, if one has a complaint against another,
forgiving each other." Every man is a burden to his neighbour and perhaps for that very reason—alas, how slow
we are to grasp the fact—a grace. He may wrong us, our
neighbour. He may really be a burden to us, and perhaps
he should not be. And yet, even such burdens should be
an extra weight of grace for a Christian. So we should bear
them, and forgive our neighbour any extra weight there
may be through his fault. The Greek term Paul uses to con-
vey this forgiveness includes the word "charis," pardon.
Accordingly he continues: "As the Lord has forgiven
you, so you also must forgive." We must forgive one
another, as the Lord has forgiven us. Or did he not have

to forgive us? Did we not need his pardon, poor sinners
that we were, whose sins, whose monstrous sins, our Lord
God had to forgive us in Jesus Christ? Why then can we
not do the same? Paul moves on, but still he thinks in the
context of this putting on of Christ: "And above all
these"—he does not repeat the words—"put on love,
which binds everything together in perfect harmony" in
the holy garment that the Christian must put on to follow
Christ. We must put on love, which is the bond of perfection. It embraces everything else, and without it nothing
is of any use. It binds everything together. We might say
that it binds everything together so stoutly that with it we
are properly girded and equipped to travel down the road
of life into the everlasting light.

Paul continues, and when he speaks of *agape,* love, he
also thinks of peace. So he says: "Let the peace of Christ
rule in your hearts" like an umpire, like a man who rules
and governs, reducing everything to order, keeping our
spiritual life running smoothly as one might say. This
deep, wholly interior peace must live and rule in our
hearts, rule over everything dark and bitter in our lives,
for those things too can be engulfed in Christ's peace.
"And", says Paul, "be thankful." We clutch avidly at God's
gifts, forgetting him himself in our desire for them. Be
thankful. "Let the word of Christ dwell in you richly, as
you teach and admonish one another in all wisdom—keep
each other right", Paul really means. Sing psalms and
hyms and spiritual songs in grace, sing God the secret song
of your heart, at least in your heart, the song of your soul,
the song that should be heard in your heart above any
merely rational thought, the song that knows only the
heart and God—this is the song you must sing in your
heart by God's grace—the unutterable melodies that the

Spirit of God can sing in your heart. It may sound to us like stammering and, as Paul says, groaning, and yet it is the sweet song we sing to God in thankfulness, the beginning of the endless praise of eternity.

"And whatever you do", Paul concludes before going on to speak of the duties of people in particular states of life, "whatever you do, in word or deed, do everything in the name of the Lord Jesus, giving thanks to God the Father through him." Everything that is right can be done in him and his name. And if it is said and done in him, then it will be right, and it will be the thanks, the eucharist—as we might say—that we owe God the Father, who has called us into the kingdom of the Son of his love so that everything in us and in our lives may praise and glorify him.

IF THE HEART IS ALIVE IT THINKS OF GOD

Col 3:12–17

(Fifth Sunday after Epiphany)

In verse 17 of this chapter in Colossians Paul says, "Whatever you do, in word or deed, do everything in the name of the Lord Jesus Christ." We must do everything, he tells us, in the name of Jesus Christ. This is what is meant when we say in the language of spirituality that we must have a good intention in whatever we do. A good intention, something good in view. Paul says: we must do everything in the name of Jesus. In the Bible the name is equivalent to the person. To speak of someone's name is to speak of his person; it conjures up the presence of the person. So when something is done in a person's name, it is done by that person's power and by his commission. Thus acting in a person's name is acting by commission from him. If we are speaking of God, this means acting in the power of his grace, in a frame of mind that is worthy of him, inspired by him; it means acting in vital union with God, with God in view, to his glory. So in everything we do or suffer, say or think, we should consider that we are commissioned by Jesus Christ our Lord: if we do or say or think a thing, it must be done in union with him and by his grace, for him, to his glory. We must remember that we belong to the sovereign Lord, that we live and die to him. Paul says in Romans 11:36 that everything is from God, exists by him and for him, and therefore concludes: To him be glory for ever. That sums up the content of our verse: because everything derives from him, is sustained by him, strives towards him with its inmost being, man must assent to this reality, must accept everything from God, do everything with and through him, everything for him. And so all is done to his glory, done in the name of our Lord Jesus Christ. If we interpret what Paul says in this way, then of course we must add that it is not enough to add that intention to what we do and say. It is an excellent thing, praiseworthy, Christian, and sanctifying, to renew our good intention frequently; for instance saying in the morning, "let everything be done to God's glory", and raising our hearts and minds to God in the course of the day's work to offer and consecrate to God whatever we are doing. But this attitude of heart, this explicit good intention, must really penetrate and fill what we do—or rather, grow out of it. If we saw things as they are and experienced human life as it is in reality, then these things, the whole of life, would tell us, as it were, that it is all from God, through God and for God. Then we would perceive the incompleteness of all that is not God, catch the deeper meaning behind things, without which they remain tentative and even pointless—much ado about nothing. Only God in things gives them their fullness, their significance, their orientation. And if we would allow outward things and our own experiences to speak of this glory of God, then our good intention would grow out of them automatically. If the bitterness of life spoke to us of beatitude, if the truth we think about spoke to us of God's eternal truth, if the mysteries and riddles of this life reminded us that God is the solution and the primal answer to all mysteries and riddles, if all trouble spoke to us of everlasting peace, all beauty of God's surpassing beauty that cannot fade, if all the love that we are given and give had God in it to keep it new and strong, then our good intention would grow out of our lives of its own accord. So we must learn to listen more attentively, and pray for a heart of flesh to perceive the mystery of God in all we do and say and think, in all we undergo, in all our loving; a heart that will say yes, will perfect, affirm, consolidate the inner movement of our life towards God, making it pure and complete, so that our daily life will be steeped in a good intention.

Of course we must agree that all this will not happen without co-operation on our part. It must be cultivated, ever and again dug up from among the rubble in which our daily life buries it, and looked after. That is why an explicit good intention is a useful and wholesome thing; stopping a moment to pray and renew our purpose of serving God. Not as though the explicit good intention were the only one. One can live to the glory of God implicitly, silently, in a general, diffuse intention that nevertheless impregnates everything. It is not just our head, our little thoughts, that must think of God but our activities, our life, all our being. And where the heart is alive, experiencing the griefs and the joys of life as they really are, where the heart has not culpably shut itself away from this authentic existence, there the heart does think of God though without so much as one explicit word. But if this is to be the case, a Christian mentality must be cultivated; we need explicit prayer, explicit recollection, we must say short prayers during the day, think consciously of God sometimes, direct our intention to our Lord Jesus Christ. And so we must often hearken to the words of St Paul: "Whatever you do, in word or deed, do everything in the name of the Lord Jesus."

Then our whole life and everything that was in it can one day be described in that line of Paul's to the Romans: Everything was from God, everything was through God, everything was for God, and so now his glory which is our blessedness, is forever.

THE ESSENCE OF CHRISTIANITY

1 Thess 1:2–10

(Sixth Sunday after Epiphany)

On the second missionary journey, when he first visited Europe, St Paul came to Salonika. Not long after founding the church there he had to move on, attacks by outsiders making it impossible for him to stay in that large and busy port. He journeyed to Athens and then on to Corinth, where he wrote this first letter to the Thessalonians some time between the years 51 and 53 A.D. When we read the opening verses of this letter, therefore, we can reflect that they are probably the first words of the New Testament to be set down in writing. And we shall notice that they contain the essential truths of the faith. Here in these few words of introduction Paul tells us, out of the plenitude of his faith, what our Christian life means. We cannot examine all Paul says here; we must select certain subjects to discuss. Let us leave aside what Paul says of his apostolic commission and of the community's apostolic work. We shall only touch on three points.

At the very beginning, in verses 2 and 3, Paul speaks of faith, hope, and love. It is only later, in the first letter to the Corinthians, that he expressly mentions these three as a special group of Christian virtues. But here we see that he is well aware of their existence. He says that Christians practise the work of faith, the labour of love, and the steadfastness of love. Now in some sense that is the whole of Christianity. When God speaks to us and calls us, and we do the work of faith throughout our lives, and if we really love God and man through this faith—do not merely feel an emotion but love them in actual deeds of sacrifice—, and if we are steadfast in hope because we know that we are pilgrims and that ultimate reality still lies ahead, if we practise this self-sacrificing love, active faith, and unshakable hope—then we are genuine Christians. Then what Paul says a few lines later of the Thessalonians can be said of us: You received the word in much affliction, with joy inspired by the Holy Spirit. In the divine Spirit that is poured forth in our hearts; we shall then be able to endure joyfully the affliction, the bitterness, the difficulties, the trials of our lives, of which Christians have not less but more than other people. For the Christian is a strange kind of person who simultaneously experiences tribulation and the joy of the Holy Ghost, which is deeper and more penetrating than any tribulation; joy that is strong and active and endures unto the end. That is the first thing St Paul says about faith, hope, and love.

The second thing that we shall note in Paul's description of Christian existence is a single word: election, *ekloge, electio*. It is a difficult word for us to hear, for us Christians of today precisely because we are Christians of today. Modern man has a way of losing himself in the crowd. He does not want to attract attention. He wants to be everyman. Now there is something to be said for this attitude. It may even be thoroughly Christian: being plain and ordinary, unobtrusive, patient with the monotony of an average, undistinguished life. Yet this odd instinct to be retiring—and it is odd—may conceal a form of cowardice. To the Christians of those other days, who were few and persecuted, whom people looked on as eccentric outsiders, Paul says: You have a vocation, you are chosen, you are called forth by God by his grace and his election. There is no need to go into the question of where others stand. Here we can apply what Jesus said to Peter: If it is my will that you follow me, why should you concern yourself with the affairs of others? Even if God saves the rest, and we can confidently commend them to his boundless mercy, our own business is to answer his call, to be convinced that he is calling us and that there is nothing for it but to follow him blindly, with no questions asked. We must realize that if we are indeed God's chosen ones, as Paul says, it means that God and his grace have done this thing, and not we ourselves. And so we must give ceaseless thanks to God, thank God always.

The third thing the Apostle speaks of is the quintessence of Christianity. He says that the Christians have turned from the idols, the false gods of their past life, to serve a living and true God; that they wait for his Son from heaven, whom he raised from the dead, until he comes again to take them into his glory, to deliver them from the wrath to come. Now that is really all Christianity is about: knowing the living, true God who has called us, who is more than all the idols of this life that we are constantly tempted to raise to altars of our hearts. For we too, just like the men of those times, are always in danger of worshipping idols, though we no longer make graven images to worship. Idols may still stand on our altars: the idol of success in this world, the idol of pleasure, the idol of recognition by men, perhaps even idols that we do not believe in, that we consider a devouring nothingness. For as well as benevolent duties men have often worshipped dark and vicious ones; and perhaps we are tempted today, in the gloom of our existence, to worship such malevolent deities. These too would count among the idols that we have been chosen to turn away from, so as to serve the true, living God, the God of everlasting life; for he has called us in Jesus Christ his Son. God's history and God's works have only just begun and we have been drawn into them, and therefore we still await the end of that holy history into which our life has been taken up, and we confess that he will come from thence to judge the living and the dead, to judge us and, we trust, everyone at the tribunal of his mercy.

There we have a few of the things Paul tells us about our Christian existence on the oldest page of the New Testament.

Let us beg God for the work of faith, the unflagging labour of love, and the steadfastness of hope; these three. If we have them, we have enough. For them we are God's chosen ones, who have turned from idols—from the idols of life—to the living God, and we wait for his Son, the eternal Word of his love which shall be spoken to us in heaven to make us happy forever.

MORALITY CANNOT JUST TICK OVER

1 Thess 4:1–7

(Second Sunday in Lent)

St Paul wrote this letter at Corinth, about the year 51 A.D., in the course of his second missionary journey, soon after he had founded the church at Thessalonica. The first part of the letter treats chiefly of his personal relations with the community, and then in chapter 4 he passes on to admonitions and to definite doctrine. The doctrine has mainly to do with the second coming of Christ. We have already discussed the first part of the section mainly devoted to morals, chapter 4, verses 1 to 7.

Paul has exhorted the Thessalonians to be upright, chaste, and honest in all they do. These things call for no special comment. But I think that when we read these admonitions, listen to them, hear them solemnly preached in church, we may find them rather a bore. To be blunt, moralizing, constant exhortation, all that sort of thing rubs us the wrong way. It may even scandalize us. Now we might give this subject a little thought.

Why does this happen? For one thing because we have so often heard it all before—in the catechism, at school, from our parents. It is ceaselessly inculcated by the spokesmen of bourgeois morality. We have heard it in the confessional, in sermons, in pastoral letters—always the same admonitions that we find Paul addressing to us today: be chaste, be honest, practise the other virtues, in short keep the ten commandments. We have heard it all so often that despite ourselves we find it a little tiresome, old-fashioned, and hackneyed. What is more, we may well reflect—and here is another stumbling-block—, this is not what Christianity is really about. Of course, these are things that must be done; agreed. But on the whole we do them, and all the exhortation is beside the point. Anyhow—we may well reflect—Christianity has to do with God, his grace, his glorious life, looking forward to eternity, the way eternity infringes on time, acknowledging the infinite, exalted, holy God of eternal life. Compared with these things—with the fact that God himself has shared our existence by becoming man in his divine Word, with the prospect of everlasting life in the company of God himself—petty moralizing really seems a little grotesque. Not that we doubt or deny those moral duties, but surely they are relatively unimportant compared with the great truths that we are taught, after all, by faith, by God's own word. After all the pedestrian morality that is so earnestly preached *is* rather obvious. What else is it but what they call the natural law, which we can discover simply by the light of reason? We are interested in God's mysteries and God's beatitude. We want to rise above this everyday morality, to know God and his eternal life, mysteries that are inaccessible to the feeble light of natural reason. And so we may even be scandalized by these admonitions.

A third reason might be adduced. All this moralizing is about *how* to live an upright life. But as to what one must actually do, what the real content of life is, the moralizers leave us none the wiser. They seem intent on restricting our lives; they point out the ditches on the right-hand of the road and on the left-hand side; but what our life and work really is, what is to content our hearts, they do not say. All these rules, these prescriptions, all this scolding, these warnings always being volunteered by unenlightened, petty-minded pedagogues and educators, do not tell us what is to be done, where our heart and mind is to find fulfilment in this life on earth.

Well, what about it? Must we be scandalized, or have we something to learn all the same when God's own word, scripture and the Church, keeps preaching these things day in, day out? Yes, God's word is right. In the first place it is marvellous what we do not happen to hear. We say we know all these rules, all these warnings, by heart; and indeed we preach them often enough ourselves to other people—to children, to adolescents, to people about us—in so many words; or at least implicitly when we think of our environment in unflattering terms. Yes, we know these rules and admonitions. But when we ought to act according to them in our own concrete life they often do not occur to us. And when they are preached, we are likely to hear everything but what speaks to our condition. We think of how the exhortation applies to others. We are always ready with an If, a But, an On the other hand, to water down God's word to us. Do we ever ask ourselves: When did I last look at the Bible, listen to a sermon, do any spiritual reading? How often do we admit with remorse and contrition: Yes, that is so; I do not act as I should? When have we really allowed ourselves to be convinced by God's word, really capitulated to his admonition and admitted that it applies to us? Man has a remarkable facility for failing to hear these rules. That is why God keeps coming with the good seed of his word, even with the seed of moral considerations, back and forth across the stony field of our heart, keeps sowing in the hope that one day something may grow there.

We must say one more thing. Morality, even ordinary morality, bourgeois morality, decency and integrity, sincerity, uprightness, are all included in true morality. Pedestrian virtues, perhaps; but, so long as they are something more than mere respectability, singularly dear to God. A man who in the inmost depths of his heart is really devoted to God's will, a man to whom God's word is law, hears a voice even in the most ordinary moral prescriptions that is the voice of his God, and not of purely human reason. A man who really and honestly obeys his conscience, not resorting to a thousand ruses to make the voice of conscience sound gentler, works for eternity in time; his humdrum days weave the fabric of a divine life. Of course these moral rules that tell us how to do things must be constantly related to the concrete content of our work, of all our earthly task. Morality cannot simply tick over on its own, as a motor idles. It is a way of doing what God has given us to do—all that we have to do in relation to our neighbour, to our work and our prayer, to our life with its joys and sorrows, to God. But if we do all that in the way God commands, then these very earthly things will become heavenly, the temporal will become eternal, and the fruit of everlasting life will grow in the field of this present time. Because that is so, because small things become great and time becomes eternity, and because it only happens if we faithfully keep God's small, perhaps awkward commandments, even when we would gladly overlook them—these admonitions in the gospels and in the letters of the apostles are meant for us as well as for the rest. We cannot bypass them to busy ourselves only with God's great glories. We must let God tell us who we have to be and what we have to be like, so that we may be true children of light, heirs of eternity, beloved brothers and sisters of the Son of God, who condescended to share our life and set us an example so that we might act like him: obedient to God's commandments and the prescriptions of morality, which are not meant to be a stumbling-block to us but a means to eternal life.

THE SUPREME CHALLENGE

Jas 1:17—21

(Fourth Sunday after Easter)

Our text for today is taken from the first chapter of the letter of St James. We might divide this chapter into two main sections, so far as this pithy letter of moral admonition can be divided at all. After the greeting, the first eighteen verses are an exhortation to steadfastness in time of temptation. Verses 19 to 27 call upon Christians to practise in their lives the gospel which they listen to in faith.

Let us consider the last few verses of this first part of St James's letter. They say: "Every good endowment and every perfect gift is from above, coming down from the Father of lights with whom there is no variation or shadow due to change"; and the next verse says: "Of his own will he brought us forth by the word of truth that we should be a kind of first fruits of his creatures."

If we would understand these verses aright, we must look at the context in which they occur. In chapter 1, verse 13 of this letter, so as to fortify us when we are faced with temptation and danger of death, St James has roundly declared that God tempts no man: God cannot be tempted with evil and he himself tempts no one; but, he goes on, each persons is tempted when he is lured and enticed by his own desire. And then sin follows. It is in this connexion that he says that every good endowment and every perfect gift is from above, coming down from the Father of lights. Now this statement may seem rather obvious. But what of St James's statement, a moment ago, that God tempts no one? It will not seem so obvious if we scan the Old and New Testaments. Does not God himself try our hearts? Is he not the Father of all things? Of all ages? Does he not hold all things in his hand? How then can anything attack us which does not come from him? How could he try our hearts if he did not lead us into temptation? Would there be any reason to pray: "Lead us not into temptation" if it were clear from the first that God does not tempt anybody? What then does the Apostle mean by saying that God tempts no one, as he himself is not tempted by evil? It is certain that God places us in this life, subjects us to trial, only because he wants our own good, wants us to be approved, wants us to receive even his gift of eternity by our own free doing in this life. He does not will darkness and evil; he does not try to involve us in sin; he places us on probation in this life so that we may have the glory of freely choosing God and eternal light. And there is no greater or more perfect gift than being allowed to do this—to be the maker, as it were, of one's own eternity, though by the grace of God. That is what God wanted man to be. That is how noble and exalted a creature God wanted him to be. And therefore however much of a temptation things may seem to be for us, all that comes from God is a good endowment, a perfect gift. It is sheer light because it comes from him. So St James says in this first verse: "Whatever comes from the Father of lights is a good endowment, a perfect gift." He means that it depends on us what happens to the sheer

light which eternal love has given us. Of course, we are
often tempted, heavy laden, provoked by evil, often in
danger of being enticed by our desire and giving birth to
sin, as St James has just said—sin that brings death with
it. Well, if that happens then we have turned God's sheer
light into darkness—so we must interpret this way God
has of dealing with man, mystery though it must always
remain. For whatever comes from him must be a good
endowment, a perfect gift. And now we ought to examine
our lives and see whether we accept all that comes to us as
God's good endowment and perfect gift, coming down
from the Father of lights who, like a changeless sun, sheds
nothing but eternal light in the empty gloom of all that is
not God.

Where is the bitterness in our life, where is the cross,
the heart-break, the enigma, the crushing burden, the
harshness, the despair? Do we stand firm against it? And
do we say, believing the Gospel: This too is a good endowment and a perfect gift from the Father of lights? This
text of St James, then, is a weighty one, a challenge to do
the greatest thing that can be done in a human life; and if
we do it, then we shall never look at anything in isolation,
so that it might become unintelligible, a provocation to sin,
a temptation. We must never look at creatures apart from
God and the intention in which he gave them to us. Only
then shall we truly see them as a good endowment, a perfect gift, and really understand what St James means when
he goes on: "Of his own will he brought us forth by the
word of truth that we should be a kind of first fruits of his
creatures." This does not mean some truth or other; this
means the truth that turns darkness into light, the cross
into a good gift, the narrowness and darkness of the creature into boundless light of God. If we accept everything

just as it comes down from God the Father of lights, if our eyes are enlightened so that we can see this light, then we are the true children of that Father of lights, begotten by the word of truth; the enlightened, adult children of God who interpret all things according to God; who have room and to spare in their hearts and can fit everything in there in due order, all the good endowments and perfect gifts; then we remain free for God, open to him, and our life remains open to God's glory; and we are really a kind of first fruits of his creatures as we are meant to be.

In many respects, I fear, we have yet to be thus brought forth by the word of truth, yet to become children of the light, a kind of first fruits of God's real creatures. The beginning was made when we were baptized and believed, but it is not yet complete; this beginning is only perfected when we ourselves have been perfected, when we have accepted everything that comes to us as a perfect gift from above, when our shadowed, mutable being, because we have thus accepted it, has entered into eternal light.

TWO PARADOXES

Jas 1:22–27

(Fifth Sunday after Easter)

Verses 22 to 27 in the first chapter of the letter of St James belong to the second part of that chapter which we have already mentioned. It is the part which tells us to be doers of the word of the Gospel and not simply hearers.

We shall select only two thoughts from today's text. Though there may be very little connexion between them, each one merits some attention.

In verse 22 St James says: "But be doers of the word, and not hearers only", and then he adds, "deceiving yourselves". The word he uses here occurs only once elsewhere in the New Testament, in Col 2:4. Literally translated, this Greek word means to "think past" a thing, to delude or beguile ourselves with all sorts of excuses, qualifications, and sophisms, as the text of Colossians says. Here James tells us to beware of thinking past reality in that way. The image he uses, if we look squarely at it, can only mean that man has the ability to shy away from hard facts, by his own fault, and thus deceive himself.

Now it is a very strange assertion to make, that man cannot only deceive others but can also deceive himself. Looking at the matter from the point of view of ordinary logic and common-sense, we might well say that such a thing is impossible. How can the deceiver and the deceived be the same person? Yet our own experience confirms what scripture tells us here, that it is indeed possible. We think of a pretence, we find it persuasive, we say we are convinced, and then we conclude that we are in good conscience. And yet we are deceivers, and we contrive to deceive ourselves.

We shall not inquire further, at the moment, into the psychology which makes such a thing possible. Let us simply learn a lesson from what St James says about talking and thinking ourselves round and past reality. Let us be suspicious of ourselves, of the many good reasons we seem to have for avoiding something unpleasant in our Christian lives, or for not honestly doing our duty, or for blaming others instead of ourselves, or envying others their apparent good fortune, or refusing to be put upon. In these and a multitude of other cases, let us heed the Apostle's warning and ask whether we are not in danger of deceiving ourselves, of guiltily distorting the knowledge that we have and suppressing the truth, as Paul says in the first chapter of Romans—God's plain, unvarnished, inexorable, perhaps humiliating truth that makes demands on us. "Do not deceive yourselves", says St James.

The second thought which we shall briefly consider today is found in verse 25 of this first chapter. Here the Apostle—he who warns us to be doers of the word and not hearers only, he who tells us later in his letter that we must not only believe but also produce the works of faith—speaks like St Paul of the perfect law of liberty. And he thinks that this idea embodies the heart of Christianity.

The perfect law of liberty: that in itself is a strange expression, well nigh a paradox. Law and freedom seem to be mutually exclusive. Where there is a law, surely, freedom ceases: and where there is freedom there surely is no law. We can gather, then, that our author is thinking of a freedom which somehow frees us by binding, and of a law which frees us by reclaiming us from a servitude in which we should otherwise be languishing and which— deceiving ourselves—we should imagine to be freedom. What St James says means something more. We human beings, one might say, by way of quasi-definition, are those strange creatures who perceive that they are finite and therefore unfree, who are prisoners of their finitude: unable to determine how long we shall live, unable to control the situation in which we find ourselves, prisoners of our limited knowledge, of the needs of our heart, of bodily sickness, of our environment, constantly exposed to death. Not only are we finite in all these ways; unlike other creatures, we know that we are finite and we feel ourselves oppressed and trapped by finitude. And along comes the Apostle talking of the perfect law of freedom.

The word "perfect" in Greek, as in English, implies that an end has been reached. The perfect law only exists complete and glorious when we ourselves have reached our end, have ceased to endure this finitude and are perfected in the unveiled freedom of God's children. Then we are wholly liberated. But James says that we are to live even now in the perfect law of liberty. And so that law must be given to us in this world, to us poor, indigent, suffering, limited, finite souls in this poor world. Yes, it is already given to us, for God's Spirit, the Spirit of infinite freedom, is already given to us—in faith, of course; in hope; and in that love which will never end. If then we feel unfree, imprisoned, distressed, and heavy laden, that is an admonition to descend deeper into our hearts, to where God already dwells in his Holy Spirit of boundless freedom. It is an admonition to pray: I believe in the perfect law of liberty, I believe in eternal life, I believe in God the liberator, in the truth of God which sets men free, in the love of God which is free. Then, doing the works of faith, we shall not feel distressed to be still in chains, because in our heart of hearts we are already liberated, and so we know that everything which still keeps us unfree is transitory, and that the perfect law of freedom endures for all eternity.

THOU ART WITH ME

1 Pet 2:21–25; Ps 23

(Second Sunday after Easter)

Today, the Second Sunday after Easter, is often known as "Good Shepherd Sunday". The reason is obvious: the Gospel of the day is in the tenth chapter of St John, verses 11 to 16; and the epistle, taken from the second chapter of First Peter, has the same theme—Christ the good shepherd. Here Christ is called the shepherd and guardian of our souls. So St Peter is echoing an expression that the Lord himself uses in St John, where he says that he is the good shepherd. The image itself comes from the Old Testament. It was usual in ancient times to call princes, those who ruled the nations, the shepherds of their people. The image was perfectly intelligible to the men of that time. They pictured a person going before his flock, feeding and guiding them, leading them to pasture, defending them, looking after them. And the men of that time modestly pictured themselves as the ones led and protected by a higher wisdom and a higher power. No one thought the image was degrading; men knew that they were in good hands; and so in the Psalms and elsewhere in the Old Testament God is called the ruler and governor of the people, the Creator and the Lord, the provident, faithful, loving, mighty prince, the shepherd of the people. And

Jesus, coming from the Father, Jesus the presence of the divine shepherd, calls himself the good shepherd. Thus he himself refers to the Old Testament; and accordingly if we would understand a little better what is said in the epistle today about the shepherd and guardian of our souls, we may quite properly go back to the Old Testament and meditate for a while on the twenty-third Psalm. It is the psalm about God our shepherd.

We all know this psalm, and yet one can read it again and again. It says: "The Lord is my shepherd." The Lord, Yahweh, he who entered into a covenant with this stiffnecked people and thought of us too as part of his people—for he had in mind the eternal covenant that we enter into, that we are called to—, the Lord who has come close to us in Jesus Christ, is our shepherd forever, the one to whom we must keep returning, as St Peter says in today's epistle. And the psalmist goes on: "I shall not want." Do we really feel that about God, the eternal and incomprehensible? Can we confidently say: "He is my shepherd whom I can trust. I belong to him. I feel his hand governing all my life. His providence watches over me. He is close to me. He feeds and guides me. I lack for nothing"? Do we not often feel quite the opposite—indigent, deprived of many things? But here the psalmist says to God: You are my shepherd, I lack for nothing. He says it calmly and boldly. He says it almost in defiance of the lessons of his life simply because it is true, though it is a truth that transcends our own experience: God is our shepherd and so we lack for nothing. So he goes on to paint what seems to be a bold, optimistic, cheerful picture of his life: "He makes me lie down in green pastures. He leads me beside still waters; he restores my soul. He leads me in paths of righteousness for his name's sake." Dear God, can we pray like this? Is this how we think of our life—resting in God's resting-places, our soul restored, led along the right path? Do we feel that God does all this, and must do it, for his name's sake, because his name is the kind and the eternal, the God of all consolation, the Almighty, the shepherd of the world—of scattered reality which must be gathered into one—, because his name is 'my shepherd'? Well, it is true, says the psalmist. For his name's sake there must be green pastures in our life where we can lie down and rest, where we can be restored and led along the right path.

Is the psalmist a foolish optimist, imagining such things? By no means. For he continues: "Even though I walk through the valley of the shadow of death"—so he has his feet on the ground, he can see human life in human terms; he is walking through the valley of the shadow of death and there seems to be no way out of it: this path that he has just called the right one, onto which the divine shepherd has led him, is the valley of the shadow of death, and it seems to get darker and darker. But he goes on: "Even though I walk through the valley of the shadow of death, I fear no evil; for thou art with me." The good shepherd accompanies us along the paths that seem dark. He is with us even where we seem to lie in darkness and the shadow of death and not in green pastures. Thou art with me. On this path the psalmist knows that he, poor little lost sheep, will be attacked by the wolves of this life, by famished vultures circling in the sky above an earth that seems to be just a graveyard; and so he remembers that the shepherd he trusts is armed with a rod and a staff to protect his flock from their enemies and get them through all the narrow passes, if need be to force them gently through; and that is why he says: "They rod"—we should say 'club'—"and they staff, they comfort me."

Can we pray this psalm about the good shepherd? Yes, we can. For when we walk in the valley of the shadow of death, there is no salvation except the words: Thou art with me even here, and it is thy rod and thy staff that comfort me.

Then the psalmist changes his image a little and as it were turns his good shepherd into a hospitable master of the house: "Thou preparest a table before me in the presence of my enemies; thou anointest my head with oil, my cup overflows. Surely goodness and mercy shall follow me all the days of my life; and I shall dwell in the house of the Lord for ever." We always dwell in the house of the Lord. We keep coming to his table, and the cup of life overflows not with gall and wormwood but with consolation and blessing, even when the case seems to be quite otherwise. Goodness and mercy, divine goodness and inexhaustible mercy shall follow me all the days of my life, says the psalmist. That is his way of telling God that he believes God is the good shepherd in Jesus Christ our Lord, the shepherd and guardian of our souls. For he has accompanied us through the darkness of this life on the way of the cross even unto Golgotha. That is why he is the good shepherd who laid down his life for us, so that we should believe that God is truly our shepherd in this life.

Shall we not say once more to him, confessing that it is our own experience: "The Lord is my shepherd, I shall not want"?

IF YOU CAN PUT UP WITH HIM,
SO CAN I

1 Pet 3:8–15

(Third Sunday after Pentecost)

If we just left this text, as it were, out of St Peter's letter, we can clearly distinguish three sections in it: one commending peace and fraternal charity; a second which confirms and reinforces the first with a rather long quotation from the thirty-third psalm; and a third which teaches that the sufferings which the just have to undergo should be accepted as a share in the sufferings of Christ.

The first thing we find in the first section, as it were the first chord struck in this exhortation to harmony and peace, is: "Have unity of spirit". Now it is an odd thing. Nowhere in scripture, neither in the Greek manuscripts nor in the Latin, is there more than the words: "Have unity of spirit". And yet the text used in the liturgy says: "Have unity of spirit in prayer". This harmony and concord, then, is interpreted to mean that we must be united in prayer. No doubt the letter of St Peter refers to a general disposition to get on with people. But we may follow the suggestion of the liturgy and take it that this concord should be expressed and embodied in prayer. This idea is obvious enough. We know only too well what a trial we are to each other. We are so different from one another: we have had different experiences, we are of different temperaments, of different origins, we come from different families, we have different talents and different jobs to do—small wonder if it is difficult for us all to be of *one* mind. We have different views and we understand each other imperfectly. And being so very different from other people we may well grate on them, unconsciously weary them with what we are, what we think, what we do, what we feel. Mutual harmony and comprehension, being of one mind, is difficult for us. Now we can only live together and bear with each other, bear one another's burdens, if we do our best to be of one mind, if we are self-effacing and self-possessed, if we can hold our tongue even when we are right, if we can let the other man be himself and give him his due, if we refrain from rash judgement and are patient. Then it becomes possible, at least in a rough and ready way, to be of one mind. We may not achieve empathy together but we can be of one mind in Christian forbearance, each bearing the other's burden. This means that I bear the burden the other man is to me simply by being himself, because I know I am a burden to him simply by being myself.

Now the liturgy says that we must be of one mind in prayer, must absorb the bitterness of discord and incomprehension into prayer: "Forgive us our trespasses, as we forgive them that trespass against us." That in itself is a kind of prayer for harmony, a kind of being of one mind in prayer, for here a man is reconciled with his brother—as today's Gospel says he must be—before bringing his gift to the altar, even if the gift is only a prayer. But we must not only pray for concord and bring a peaceable, forbearing heart to our prayer; we must also take our fellow-man into our prayer and so make the prayer come true. Often we are not of one mind simply because we are so different from each other. How then can we achieve unity of spirit? Only in God, who is the one goal of the most diverse things and the most diverse men; only in God, in whom we live and move and have our being, is that unity possible. And we are in God only when we are praying. Could we not sometimes try taking our neighbour with us to God—the man who gets on our nerves so, who annoys us with everything he is and does, who seems to be so unfair to us, so unsympathetic, so heartless? Could we not say to God: Here is the man I cannot manage to get on with. He belongs to you. You made him. If you do not will him to be the way he is, at least you allow him to be that way. Dear God, I want to put up with him the way you put up with me. Would we not find our heart a little lighter, more at ease, more patient? And then if we knew that somebody else was really praying for us, if we knew that he was not just talking, mouthing pious platitudes, but taking his heart to the feet of God, daring to speak to that sacred majesty that never dies, to say with all his heart, with the audacity one can only have in Christ Jesus: "Our Father, who art in heaven"; to say to him: "My God, my Lord, my Redeemer, my compassion, my eternity, my love", and then if he should take me into such a prayer and commend me to his God, would not something ineffable happen? Could I go on feeling bitter towards him if in that sanctuary, with patience and tenderness, he had spoken lovingly to his God about me?

I think being at one in prayer does have a meaning. Only if we become more and more at one in prayer, shall we be worthy of God's eternal kingdom, for that kingdom is the kingdom of those who are eternally diverse and eternally at one in the love of one God.

TO BE SOBER AND YET TO LOVE

1 Pet 4:7–11

(Sunday within the octave of the Ascension)

If we preface today's epistle with a brief passage from St Peter's letter and append another brief passage to it in the spirit of this letter, then we shall have a complete pericope. We shall begin with the statement: "The end of all things is at hand", and end with the verse: "To him be the dominion for ever and ever. Amen."

Let us briefly consider this text together, just as it comes. From chapter 3 onwards Peter speaks of certain motives for leading the Christian life he has commended in the preceding chapters. He cites the example of the Crucified; he speaks of our dying with Christ and then—here today's passage begins—he thinks of the day of judgement: The end of all things is at hand.

That is always so. It is so no matter how long the history of the world may go on. For our life, our brief and finite life, impinges directly on the eternal God. It is temporal; it is ordered to an end; and the distance between what now is and the end, is inconsiderable. The end is at hand. We live only once and irrevocably; we do not know how much time is left to us. We do not know whether we are young or old. We must look beyond our fleeting life; for as the letter to the Hebrews says, it is appointed for men to die once, and after that comes judgement. This thought prompts St Peter to give us two guiding principles for our life: We are to keep sane and sober, and love one another.

Now one might suppose that only the former of these two principles followed from the fact that the end is nigh. If one knows that everything will soon be over, then of course it is well to be sober; then our whole life in this world, everything that we have done and suffered, everything that has delighted us or busied us, ceases to be trivial: it all assumes an enormous importance; it becomes weighty simply because it was once lived and because our life is lived out within so small a compass; it is all relative, but in the literal sense—related to the end, to eternity, to the judgement, to the ultimacy of our existence. Then one is sober; for he who contemplates and weighs things as they are, as the Imitation says, is both sober and watchful and, as St Peter goes on, knows how to pray. For when can one pray? When contemplating God, when grasping the reality and earnestness of life, realizing that all we are and have and experience is ordered with deadly certainty to God's judgement. Then one holds out one's life, one's heart, one's joys, and one's sorrows to God; then one prays. It is less easy to understand why the Apostle connects the end of all things with the admonition: "Above all hold unfailing your love for one another." And yet a man can really love only if he is free of himself, only when he has anchored his mind and his life in God. Only then can he look at things from outside himself, only then can he truly love; and it is perfectly true that those who truly love their neighbour also love God, even if they are not aware of the fact. Be that as it may, anyone who knows the span of his life in God and faces it in God is free of himself and able to love his neighbour. "Above all hold unfailing your love for one another", says St Peter. And then he says something, something consoling, that must have been a familiar saying in ancient Christianity, that Peter did not invent himself, that is based on a saying in the Old Testament, that occurs in St James and elsewhere in early Christian literature. He says: "Love covers a multitude of sins." If we feel that we are sinners, if we find ourselves wanting in many respects and falling daily, let us say to encourage and console ourselves: Love covers a multitude of sins. It is almost as if scripture were being vague and lax; but that is what it says; and we may take it on God's word.

What else? "Practise hospitality ungrudgingly to one another." In the conditions then prevailing this was a very important and practical admonition, which may seem less important to us now that there are so many hotels and restaurants. And yet it may be that we now live in greater isolation than ever; perhaps our ability to make contact, as they say, is less than ever. Well, we should at least seek out our neighbour spiritually and entertain him spiritually, take his worries and difficulties and joys into our inner man; then he will more easily find his way to our house and our table and will perceive that there he has a home and a country of his own in the love of Christ.

Next Peter considers men in their variety and says to them—and really this is another source of consolation for us—that each should love the other with the gifts that he has. Not every one has every gift, and so we cannot all be useful to each other in every possible respect. Certainly we cannot give many people all the help they need. God meant somebody else to do the rest, without a doubt. What we have to do—it is a consolation and an admonition—is serve our neighbour with our own gift, small as it may be, odd as it may be. Serve one another with the gift of grace that each one has received. God often does not require what we imagine he requires for the service of our neighbour; but he bluntly demands that we use the gift he has given us.

Let us ask ourselves: what talents have I that I may be hiding away in a napkin like the unprofitable servant in the Gospel, not allowing them to benefit others because I am self-centred, because I love my ease, because I want to be left in peace, because I do not want to serve as the Apostle tells us to? St Peter makes another application of the same ideal. Perhaps he is thinking of the Church's priests and deacons when he says: "Whoever renders service, let him render it by the strength which God supplies." However that may be, we must take our orders, and then we hear the consoling reminder: no more is expected of you than what you are able to do, whatever the distress of the world and even of your neighbour may be. Only be sure you use your gift in the strength which God supplies, in God's sight, on God's errand, in his grace, with him in view, as a man responsible to him, so that you may serve your brother, thus truly loving him, and stand firm when the end of everything has come.

In that spirit St Peter concludes this passage: "So may God be glorified in everything through Jesus Christ." The motto of the Benedictines, *Ut in omnibus honorificetur Deus,* is taken from this epistle. It could well be our motto: In everything I experience, think, do, or suffer, and in my dying, may God be glorified through Jesus Christ who lives in us, who has given us his strength to live and die with, so that in us too the Son may be glorified before the Father. Peter closes: "To him be the dominion for ever and ever.

Amen." That is the end of all that Peter wishes to say to us today, all that our life should say: To him who alone is blessed, to the great and everlasting God of our life, be dominion in our Lord, in the power of the Holy Ghost who is poured forth in us, for ever and ever.

WHY ARE WE HATED?

1Jn 3:13–18

(Second Sunday after Pentecost)

The third chapter of St John's first letter, especially the first part, is devoted to brotherly love. Today's text is drawn from that chapter. Let us simply consider verse 13 for a moment. There we read: "Do not wonder, brethren, that the world hates you." If we look at the context within which this verse is to be seen, we find the following: We should love one another, and not be like Cain who was of the evil one and murdered his brother. We must not be people who hate others because we cannot endure goodness. And then, in this connexion, he says without any apparent need: "Do not wonder that the world hates you." According to John love, kindness, holiness, and justice arouse hatred; and because this is so, because astonishingly the Apostle takes the fact for granted, he says: "Do not wonder that the world hates you." He assumes that Christians are people who do good works, like Abel. So John thinks that goodness and justice provoke the antagonism, anger, and hatred of the unjust man, because he cannot endure the contrast with himself; he wants to see his actions endorsed by the actions of others, and is forced to blame himself and disavow himself if he encounters another man whose deeds are just and good, so good that the man even loves his evil fellow-man. So goodness stirs up malice, love stirs up hatred and justice injustice. Injustice comes to light and is exposed because it cannot bear goodness. Now John says that this must happen to us; he admonishes us not to be surprised when it does happen to us. Of course the warning shows that we need to be rallied and encouraged to face this strange experience of good stirring up evil in this world which is divided and on trial, this world where man is asked to choose between good and evil, loving and hating, justice and injustice. But it seems to me that we have an altogether different reason for being surprised at this verse of scripture. Does our heart need to be strengthened against the hatred which St John says the world bears us? Let us be perfectly frank. Can we say that the world hates us? Are we persecuted for being Christians? Do we suffer violence and impoverishment for conscience' sake? Can we say that we do not belong to this world and therefore feel the lash of its hatred? Or must we say: No, to be honest we are no better off than many other countries, we have our difffculties and perhaps our tragedies, but we cannot really pretend that the world hates us because we are just, because we love those who hate us. Now if such is the case, are we what we really should be, people that St John can assume will be hated by the world and who must be admonished not to wonder at that hatred? When we read this passage we ought to wonder, indeed be alarmed, that we are getting on so well in this country. We must ask whether we are the Christians we should be. By this standard of real Christianity we may well find ourselves wanting before God and our conscience. Were we strictly faithful to what we know is right, were we whole-heartedly on the side of the Gospel, had we not taken this world of hatred and injustice into ourselves and given it room there, perhaps we should be less popular, perhaps we should realize more keenly that we are different from the children of this world. Of course we are in danger of misapplying this criterion which shows our Christianity in such an unflattering light. There are Christians who think that to stand against the world would simply be old-fashioned and reactionary. There are Christians who come into conflict with non-Christians and rightly so, because the latter do not object to real Christianity but to the un-Christian ways of us Christians, because we are a stumbling block to non-Christians instead of being the men we should be, so that others confuse us with our religion and conclude—alas—that they must reject our religion because they are rightly dissatisfied with ourselves.

In such cases we dare not say: We must not wonder that the world hates us. No. We should indeed wonder, not at others but at ourselves. All the same, this gives us no right to condemn everything about the Church, Catholic practice, and Christianity as inadequate, out-of-date, reactionary, or even false, simply because it does not meet with the approval of the world. For here we are told: "Do not wonder that the world hates you." Do not wonder either if this hatred, this bitter hostility towards everthing Christian, holy, divine, and Catholic, masquerades under the pretext that only what is old-fashioned, reactionary, musty, and primitive is being attacked. We ought not to wonder at the hatred of the world, even this concealed hatred, which can be a real hatred and must only confirm us in our faith. So this world really places us in a strange position. We must not wonder at the hostility of the world, but wonder that there is so little hostility towards us. We must not provoke it with anything that is not the pure and genuine Christianity of love, truth, and fidelity to conscience. In other words, in ourselves and in the world we must constantly discern the Christian spirit from the un-Christian spirit. That is difficult. We need the light of God, a fidelity and a purity of conscience that is able to criticize ourselves and criticize the world. A staggering task. We must keep asking ourselves whether we are not much like mankind in general, whether we are not—in St Paul's phrase—too much conformed to this world. We must keep asking whether we do not misrepresent Christianity and give scandal to those who are not Christians but quite possibly are in search of true Christianity, because we pretend to be Christians and are nothing of the kind. May God give us the grace to bear the real hatred of the world with courage and equanimity, steadfast in our own genuine Christianity; and may God give the Church of today and her hierarchy, and each one of us in his own life, the grace not to make Christianity seem to the world unworthy of credence through our own fault.

SEALED WITH THE SEAL OF EVERLASTING LOVE

Apoc 7:2–12

(All Saints' Day)

It is common knowledge how difficult and mysterious the Revelation of St John seems to be. But much of the obscurity is only apparent. If we realize the kind of language that is used here, we can much more easily distinguish between the imagery and what the image means. The seer is looking into his own time and into his Christian life; and enlightened by the Spirit of God and his own Christian experience, he looks into the future and sees as far as the end. He sees his present and the future of Christianity in a single perspective, as it were. He is not a reporter, relating one event after another in chronological order; we cannot apply the particular things he says to any definite historical events in the future. Rather, he keeps seeing one and the same thing in massive imagery—the crucial struggle that goes on throughout the history of the world and ends in eternal victory for God, when the eternal kingdom has been established and God has triumphed in his Christ, gathering together all that was scattered in time into his eternal glory. This one thing is said over and over again. When the seer has admonished, warned, and corrected seven Christian communities of Asia Minor in the first few chapters of this book, he presents the first great image: He sees the eternal

God and he sees that God is holding a book in his hand, a book sealed with seven seals. It is the book of universal history, the book of creation and time. What this book contains is really the history of the world, the history of salvation and damnation. Nobody can break the seals of this book or scroll, except the Lamb that was slain, the Crucified, the Son of God, who is the meaning of history, who came into history and experienced and suffered all that has ever happened, as the crucified and risen Lord. And when a voice asks: Who is worthy to open the scroll and break its seals?, and when nobody is found and the seer weeps because no one knows the meaning of all that we experience, then he hears a voice saying: Weep not; for the Lamb that was slain, the victor, can break the seven seals of the universal history which God alone can write; he opens this history. Now, continuing the same imagery, the seven seals are broken, one after another, and the same universal history is revealed from beginning to end each time, only in a different perspective; with its plagues, its disasters, and that great silence that falls when the end comes. In the same terms the seer sees the designation of God's chosen ones. He sees it in two ways: under the figure of the twelve tribes—which simply means all mankind; for we are dealing with the spiritual Israel, the whole human race which is called to God's eternal glory. And he sees an immense multitude that no man could count, of every race and nation and language. He sees them as having already made their way through history and as beginning their eternal praise of the holy God. He sees those who are sealed, and sees them as sealed before the history of the world with its plagues really begins. They are those who are called and chosen by God's decree. This decree is the primal thing, and all the rest—universal history—is only its consequence, fitted into the decree and destined to glorify God. The seer sees God's angel sealing the elect: from every tribe and people and tongue, from everywhere in universal history, God gathers those whom he loves. There is no question of his leaving anybody out. We are simply told that he calls and chooses his elect from everywhere to sign and seal them as his own, the possession that he perfects, saves, and keeps through all this history. And since we are told that there are many, a great multitude which no man could number, we may hope that we too are among them and that what seems to be said here in such general terms is said of us, of you and me. We hope that we are among them, bearing God's seal invisible on our forehead, that each one of us is already sealed as he makes his way through his own whole history; and that if we were seers and could see all that is to be unto the end, we should catch sight of ourselves there before the throne of God and the Lamb, hear ourselves singing praises there as we shall do one day.

This is how we must interpret today's text. We must apply it to ourselves, to each one of ourselves, to those we love, to the dead who are alive and to the living, to those who are with us in Christ and those on whom God can and does have mercy in other ways: for by God's grace all of these can be sealed. Often as we must fear for our own salvation, we have no right to exclude anyone from the hope of eternal life. So we can—we who are commanded to hope—, we can and must apply today's text to everyone, to ourselves and to all the rest of mankind. Then we remember those who have gone before us in the sign of faith and who sleep the sleep of peace, and we believe that they too are sealed; and we think of our fellow-pilgrims, at our side, or a little ahead of us, or a little behind us. Soon all these differences will be no more: we are all on pilgrimage to eternity. God calls us all, and we hope that all too are sealed.

That is the seer's vision of human history and of our own lives. As we listen to this reading from God's word, we should apply St John's vision to the personal experience of history we have had, the experience of death and pain, the experience of the pitiful poverty of human life, and the experience of its grandeur. We should hear the weeping and the laughter, the deep things men say and the superficial things that seem to be ceaselessly gabbled millennium after millennium. We should apply anything that strikes us in this universal history written today, on All Saints' Day, for us and for everyone, written as it were before God rings up the curtains, as it were before he lets loose the angels of history to do their work which seems so baffling and senseless. Before we look into the book of universal history with its seven seals, we should be told that God has sealed those he calls into history, with the mark of his love. Then that history can be endured. It is obscure, and one might almost say that God should rather give us an account of our life than call us to account for it; for he is God and must therefore answer for our existence. But he has told us—and what other answer could there be for us in time, in this imperfect life, upon our shadowed journey—, he has told us that he has sealed us with the seal of his eternal love and that he sends down no road that will not lead to him, puts us into no history that will not end in his beatitude, calls no one into existence who is not chosen and sealed with God's eternal love. On All Saints' Day and All Souls' Day we remember those who have learnt that they are sealed and called and we raise our eyes in faith and hope to our own blessed end.